Japan's Lost Decade

Japan's Lost Decade

Origins, Consequences and Prospects for Recovery

Edited by
Gary R. Saxonhouse and Robert M. Stern

Blackwell
Publishing

350 Main Street, Malden, MA 02148-5018, USA
108 Cowley Road, Oxford OX4 1JF, UK
550 Swanston Street, Carlton, Victoria 3053, Australia

First published 2004 by Blackwell Publishing Ltd

Library of Congress Cataloging-in-Publication Data

ISBN 1-4051-1917-9

A catalogue record for this title is available from the British Library.

Set by Graphicraft Limited, Hong Kong

For further information on
Blackwell Publishing, visit our website:
http://www.blackwellpublishing.com

Contents

1 The Bubble and the Lost Decade
GARY R. SAXONHOUSE and ROBERT M. STERN   1

2 Retrospective on the Bubble Period and its Relationship to Developments
in the 1990s
TAKATOSHI ITO.   17

3 Why Does the Problem Persist? 'Rational Rigidity' and the Plight of
Japanese Banks
KIYOHIKO G. NISHIMURA and YUKO KAWAMOTO   35

4 Japan's Fiscal Policies in the 1990s
TOSHIHIRO IHORI, TORU NAKAZATO and MASUMI KAWADE   59

5 Japan's Negative Risk Premium in Interest Rates: The Liquidity Trap
and the Fall in Bank Lending
RISHI GOYAL and RONALD McKINNON   73

6 Japan's Lost Decade and its Financial System
MITSUHIRO FUKAO   99

Index   119

1

The Bubble and the Lost Decade

Gary R. Saxonhouse and Robert M. Stern

1. INTRODUCTION

A LITTLE more than a dozen years ago, in 1989, Japan was completing a decade of excellent economic performance. Its 3.9 per cent average annual rate of growth of gross domestic product, while slower than what it had achieved in any earlier decade since 1950, was still significantly better than the performance of the world's other advanced industrialised economies. During this same decade, equity prices rose six-fold and land prices more than four-fold.[1]

Even as equity and land prices increased dramatically, in 1989, many economists were prepared to argue that the new valuations were justified by Japan's economic fundamentals.[2] Japan's distinctive, but superior system of economic management, both at the government level and within the firm, it was argued, justified more optimistic expectations of further exceptional economic growth even as Japan's unusually high national savings rate kept real interest rates lower than those in other major industrialised economies. Indeed, its distinctive economic system was seen as working so well by comparison with those of other major economies that Japan was hailed by Chalmers Johnson (1989) as the only 'Communist nation that works.'

In March 2002, when the Symposium was convened in Ann Arbor at which earlier versions of the chapters in this book were presented, Japan looked very different. Japan's post-1989 GDP growth has averaged no more than 1.2 per cent annually, worse than that of any other major industrialised country. Japan's equity markets, after reaching a peak at the end of 1989, have fallen by 75 per cent.

GARY R. SAXONHOUSE and ROBERT M. STERN are from the University of Michigan (Ann Arbor). The papers in this issue were prepared initially for a Symposium held on 22 March, 2002, at the University of Michigan. Support was provided by the Japan Foundation, Centre for Global Partnership. The latter stages of Saxonhouse's work on this project were facilitated by a residency at the Rockefeller Foundation's Bellagio Study and Conference Center.

[1] See Figure 1 in Takatoshi Ito's Symposium paper below.
[2] Frankel (1991) reviews much of this literature.

Japanese land prices have fared still worse with prices falling by 80 per cent, so that in 2002, Japanese land prices are below levels prevailing 20 years ago. Thus, Chalmers Johnson, contradicting his earlier analysis, more recently (1998) has written that 'Japan truly fits the crony capitalism description that has complacently continued to protect its structurally corrupt and sometimes gangster-ridden firms.' As Nishimura and Kawamoto show in their Symposium paper below, the very economic institutions, such as community banking and permanent employment (and they might have added close government-business relationships) that for four decades were seen as enhancing Japanese growth prospects are now seen as standing in the way of renewed superior economic performance.

With hindsight, it is easy to criticise the failure of so many observers in the late 1980s to foresee the marked change that was about to occur in Japan's economic fortunes. In light of the experience of the United States in the 1990s, however, it is clear that such failures are not unique to Japan. In both Japan in the late 1980s and in the United States in the late 1990s, prices of assets, such as equities and land, rose rapidly even while the prices of goods and services were relatively stable. In such an environment, it admittedly is difficult to determine, until after the fact, whether the asset-price increases represent speculative excess or a secular change in the rate of growth of productivity. But, for our purposes, we will assume that a *bubble* did occur in Japan. With this in mind the Symposium that follows seeks to explore: (1) whether *the bubble* could have been prevented; (2) how much of the economic pain that Japan faced during the 1990s was the result of *the bubble*'s collapse; and (3) what can be done today to help resolve Japan's continuing economic problems.[3]

2. COULD THE BUBBLE HAVE BEEN PREVENTED?

Takatoshi Ito addresses the first of the issues raised above in his Symposium paper. Mindful that it is difficult to know that a bubble has occurred until after it is over, Ito suggests that the Bank of Japan (BOJ), at the time of the Louvre Accord in February 1987, should not have cut the discount rate from 3 to 2.5 per cent. Failing that, he argues that the BOJ discount rate could still have been raised in August 1988 when the Federal Reserve and the Bundesbank raised interest rates. According to Ito, earlier tightening of monetary policy might have nipped *the bubble* in the bud, but even in the summer of 1988 tightening credit conditions might still have prevented some of the worst problems that ultimately arose. By May 1989 when the discount rate was finally raised, according to Ito, it was too late.

---

[3] These and other current issues pertinent to Japan are also explored in depth in the papers in Stern (2003).

To underline how politically difficult it might have been for the BOJ to raise its discount rate, it should be remembered that, during the very years that Ito says that the BOJ should have reversed policy, many observers abroad were not only praising Japan's economic institutions, they were also praising the quality of Japanese macroeconomic management for simultaneously keeping interest rates low and inflationary expectations damped. For example, David Hale, a highly influential US business economist, wrote in August 1989 that:

> During the second half of the decade, it was the Japanese MOF [Ministry of Finance] which used a mixture of direct intervention and moral suasion to protect the US financial system from sharply rising interest rates at a time when foreign private investors lost confidence in the US dollar.

> ... the MOF and the BOJ pursued a low interest rate policy to boost the US dollar during 1987–88 and neutralized the potential inflationary consequences on credit growth through administrative guidance (pp. 60–61).

Likewise, in 1988, C. Fred Bergsten, the Director of the Institute for International Economics, praised Japanese policies:

> Since 1986, in perhaps its most impressive performance to date, Japan has adjusted to a near doubling in the dollar value of the yen by shifting with remarkable speed from the export-led growth of the early 1980s to a domestic-led expansion that has produced a burst of rapid growth despite the steady decline of its trade balance in real terms.

> Japan's new Five-Year Plan (1988–92) projects GNP growth of 3.75 percent annually and growth in domestic demand of 4.25 percent annually. ... It ... seems both desirable and feasible for Japan to exceed targets in the plan, perhaps maintaining domestic demand at about 6 percent annually. In fact, domestic demand growth reached an estimated 7.4 percent in 1988 (pp. 63 and 103).

Quite apart from an earlier move to more restrictive macroeconomic policies, Ito suggests that stricter prudential policies, had they been adopted, could have had a significant impact on the magnitude of *the bubble*. Ito believes that Japanese authorities could have: (1) introduced a regulation (or guidance) on the loan/value ratio on real estate lending, citing the increased risk of real-estate-price volatility; and (2) issued a regulation (or guidelines) to limit lending to real-estate-related sectors, citing the risks of concentrating loans too heavily in a single sector.

Many market participants in the late 1980s already recognised that these very steps, that Ito now recommends with hindsight, were required. Interestingly enough, they believed that the Japanese government was taking just such measures. Quoting again from Hale:

> The BOJ ordered the banks to reduce the growth rate of total lending and sharply curtailed the supply of funds available for property speculation. As a result, the growth rate of bank lending for real estate fell from 32% to 8% and there was a modest decline in Tokyo real estate prices during 1987 and 1988 despite a monetary policy which was highly accommodating in every

other respect. The MOF also used restrictions on land availability to prevent the slowdown in property lending from producing a price collapse[4] (p. 62).

After rising rapidly from 8 to 13 per cent between 1980 and 1986, loans to the real estate sector as a percentage of total loans to Japan's city banks, as Hale suggests, did not increase further. This was insufficient, however, to puncture the nation-wide land bubble.[5] It was only in 1990 when the BOJ capped total loans and, not just their proportion to total lending, that *the bubble* began to show signs of bursting.

3. THE BUBBLE AND JAPAN'S PROBLEMS IN THE 1990s

Whether *the bubble* could have been prevented is one issue. To what extent it was responsible for the host of the problems that the Japanese economy faced during the 1990s and continues to face today is another. The Symposium papers are in agreement that the equity and real estate bubble's bursting need not have caused a dozen years of travail for Japan. With a different set of policies, Japan might have recovered in a few years' time.

a. Ineffective Fiscal Policy

In their Symposium paper, Ihori, Nakazato and Kawade blame the prolonged recession and slow recovery on the macroeconomic measures pursued by the MOF. Neither government spending nor tax cuts did much to stimulate the economy. These findings are particularly interesting because recent influential work by Kuttner and Posen (2001), like Ihori et al., use vector auto regressions (VAR) to do their analysis of Japanese fiscal policy, but unlike Ihori et al., conclude that, when used, fiscal policy was effective.[6] While Kuttner and Posen blame the Lost Decade on insufficient use of fiscal measures, Ihori et al. find fiscal policy

---

[4] While Hale's numbers may surprise some, his bank-lending statistics are from those of the BOJ, while his Tokyo real-estate-price data are taken from the official National Land Agency series. See also Figure 2 below in the Nishimura and Kawamoto Symposium paper. Writing in mid-1989, Hale did not know that whatever success the BOJ had in restraining bank lending in 1987 and 1988 was not matched in 1989 when bank loans for real estate grew at 14.7 per cent and when Tokyo land prices once again started rising. Werner (2002) characterises Japanese government policy in exactly the opposite way from Hale. Werner argues that the BOJ used 'window guidance' to push a reluctant Japanese banking sector to continue to extend new loans to the real estate sector.
[5] Nihon sorifu (1995). Unlike Tokyo, nationally land prices continued to increase throughout 1987 and 1988.
[6] R. Glenn Hubbard (2002), the Chairman of the Council of Economic Advisers, cites the fiscal policy results of Kuttner and Posen. Ramaswamy and Rendu (2000) and Walker (2002) come to conclusions generally in accord with those of Ihori et al.

becoming ineffective in the 1990s as concerns about the size of Japan's public debt grew. Some of the differences in findings between Kuttner and Posen and Ihori et al. can be attributable to differences in the data sets being used. Kuttner and Posen used annual data and assumed that macroeconomic relationships that held before and during *the bubble* also held in the 1990s.[7] In contrast, Ihori et al. used quarterly data and therefore have enough observations to allow relationships in the 1990s to be different from those prevailing earlier.[8]

b. The Domestic Consequences of International Finance

While Ihori et al. focus exclusively on macroeconomic policy in attempting to make sense of what happened to Japan in the 1990s, the Symposium papers by Goyal and McKinnon and by Fukao look more directly at the interaction between microeconomic and macroeconomic issues. The bursting of *the bubble* in 1990 and thereafter meant that many of the loans made in the 1980s to the real estate sector by Japanese banks could not be repaid. Japanese banks, the BOJ, and the MOF were slow to publicly acknowledge the scale of this problem. A quick write-off of these non-performing loans would have left most Japanese banks too thinly capitalised (or worse) to continue operations without a new infusion of capital. Given the uncertain environment and the lack of reliable information about the financial condition of Japan's banks, this capital infusion could only come from the Japanese Government. But for much of the decade the use of public money in this way to bail out Japan's banks was politically impossible.

In contrast to the position taken by Ito, both Goyal and McKinnon and Fukao emphasise that, given the small spread in the 1990s between loan rates and deposit rates, such an infusion of capital would have failed. While these two papers reach similar conclusions, their analyses are quite different. Goyal and McKinnon note that for much of the past 25 years interest rates on Japanese loans tended to move

---

[7] Kuttner and Posen include a linear time trend and a trend interacted with a post-1990 dummy in their model.

[8] Tamim Bayoumi, in commenting on the Ihori et al. paper when it was presented in Ann Arbor, argued that quarterly national income accounts in Japan are not very reliable. As evidence, Bayoumi noted: (1) the standard deviation of the consensus forecast among business economists is high; (2) Japanese equity markets rarely respond to the release of quarterly national-income-account data; and (3) the quarterly national-income-accounts data in Japan are subject to unusually large revisions. But, it may be noted, Japan's annual national-income-accounts data, particularly the government fiscal data, are also fraught with many of the same problems as the quarterly accounts and are viewed by many as not giving an accurate picture of government behaviour. See Ando (2002). Using quarterly national-income-accounts data, in the context of the FRB/Global Market Model, Ahearne et al. (2002) come to conclusions about the efficacy of fiscal policy similar to those of Kuttner and Posen. However, it should be pointed out that the VAR methods of the sort used by both Ihori et al. and Kuttner and Posen are a response to criticism that macroeconometric models such as the FRB/Global are not overidentified as their builders commonly assumed. This critique is contained in the seminal paper by Sims (1980).

in tandem with US interest rates even while always maintaining a substantial negative differential. For the period up until 1995, Goyal and McKinnon attribute this pattern to relatively stable expectations of a continuing increase in the value of the yen relative to the dollar.[9] Since 1995 even as these expectations have evaporated, this differential has persisted, reflecting the premium that the heavily-indebted United States has to pay creditor nations to bear the exchange risk associated with holding dollar-denominated debt.

According to Goyal and McKinnon, as long as interest rates in the United States were relatively high, the negative differential between the US and Japanese interest rates did not pose special and unique problems for the conduct of economic policy in Japan. As interest rates have fallen in the United States, however, Japanese interest rates have increasingly been pushed towards zero and into a liquidity trap.[10] With interest rates near zero, monetary policy has lost its effectiveness as a means of economic recovery. Since the early 1990s substantial increases in bank reserves have not gone hand-in-hand with substantial increases in bank credit to the private sector. With compressed lending rates and the zero lower bound on deposit rates, and hence with low profit margins on new commercial lending, Goyal and McKinnon emphasise that banks have an incentive to change their portfolio allocation away from commercial lending into low transaction-cost government bonds. In this low profit-margin environment, unlike US banks in the early 1990s, the Japanese banks cannot gradually re-capitalise themselves after writing off their non-performing loans. Nor, in this environment, will an injection of capital from the Japanese Government make Japanese banks any more likely to be more aggressive in extending loans.[11]

c. Deregulation, Corporate Governance, and Government-sponsored Financial Institutions

Unlike Goyal and McKinnon, Fukao maintains that macroeconomic considerations are insufficient to account for the small difference between loan rates and deposit rates in Japan. It is hardly surprising that commercial lending is unattractive at a rate comparable to that of long-term bonds. The question is why commercial banks did not raise their loan rates to make such lending more profitable for them. Fukao attributes this to competition that the commercial banks faced from government-sponsored financial institutions on the one hand and governance problems on the other.[12]

---

[9] This argument is developed in McKinnon and Ohno (1997).
[10] Krugman (1998) was the first to develop and popularise the analysis that Japan might be in a liquidity trap.
[11] On moral hazard grounds, it is possible to argue that the reverse will be the case.
[12] Goyal and McKinnon explicitly reject the view that it is competition from government-sponsored financial institutions that is responsible for the low margins of Japan's commercial banks.

In Japan, government-sponsored financial institutions have about 25 per cent of the loan market, 33 per cent of the deposit market and 40 per cent of the life insurance market. Their loan rates are similar to those of private commercial banks, but their loans usually have longer maturities and government-sponsored financial institutions typically accept early repayment without penalty. According to Fukao, the terms of the loans being offered by government-supported financial institutions do not make them profitable. But since these institutions receive about one trillion yen per year in direct and indirect subsidies, this is not a problem for them.

Even if commercial banks did not face competition from government-sponsored financial institutions, Fukao argues that they would have great difficulty operating profitably in Japan's deregulated environment in which the MOF no longer provides banks with regulatory rents.[13] Commercial banks do not face strong pressures from shareholders to operate efficiently. The commercial banks' largest shareholders are mutual-life-insurance companies. Mutual-life-insurance companies do not have shareholders. Management is supposedly accountable to its policy holders, but with the policy holders' representatives selected by management, Fukao concludes that there is no accountability at all and no incentives in place for insurance companies to use resources efficiently and demand high return on the investments that they do make.[14] This lack of pressure on the management of the commercial banks' principal stockholders, in turn, insulates the commercial banks' management from governance pressure to stop unprofitable lending activities. Like Goyal and McKinnon, Fukao believes that Japanese banks suffer from more than a bubble-attributable bad loan problem. If bad loans were the only problem facing commercial banks, a capital infusion might be enough to solve the problem. Given competition from government-sponsored financial institutions and the governance problems facing commercial banks, even after a round of capital infusion like that in 1999, allowing older non-performing loans to be written off, the continuing absence of operating profits, not to mention the emergence of new non-performing loans, means that a new round of infusions will soon be required according to Fukao.

d. Community Banking and Structural Change

Unlike Fukao, Nishimura and Kawamoto do not see the Japanese banking system's long-standing failure to write off non-performing loans as a corporate governance issue. Rather they view Japanese commercial banks as having throughout the last half

---

[13] It was these rents that allowed Japanese commercial banks to compete successfully with government-sponsored financial institutions from the early 1950s to the late 1980s.
[14] Banks and the mutual-life-insurance companies with which they are allied raise capital from one another, creating the false illusion that their balance sheets are far stronger than is actually the case.

century operated according to a community-banking business model. The traditional financial *keiretsu* view that emphasises the relationship between Japanese banks and large corporations, according to Nishimura and Kawamoto, cannot explain the reluctance of Japanese banks to write off non-performing loans made to small and medium-size enterprises.[15] This is an important issue because almost half the loans made by Japanese banks are to such firms.

Reasoning by analogy with Japanese labour-management practices, Nishimura and Kawamoto see Japanese commercial banks as seeking long-term relationships, not only with larger firms, but with all their commercial borrowers.[16] This leads them to eschew short-term profit maximisation in favour of maximising profits over the lifetime of the firm. For Nishimura and Kawamoto, the community-banking business model provides a rational explanation for why commercial banks continue to offer loan rates that are unprofitable for them and why commercial banks continue to lend to firms that are in default on their repayments.

Nishimura and Kawamoto recognise that the community-banking business model was a product of a period when the Japanese economy was expanding relatively rapidly and when asset prices were rising. Given that this was a characteristic of Japan for 40 years prior to 1990, it is hardly surprising that practices of community banking became institutionalised and are difficult to change in what is now a very different environment.

4. RESOLVING JAPAN'S ECONOMIC PROBLEMS

The problems that Japan faces today are still worse than they were earlier in the Lost Decade. To cite only two examples: (1) the public debt outstanding as a percentage of GDP is orders of magnitude higher than it was in the early 1990s; and (2) commercial bank balance sheets while already weakened in the early 1990s are far weaker today. The Symposium papers make many recommendations as to what needs to be done to bring Japan out of its long-standing recession. From the perspective of a decade ago, what is remarkable is that no one is recommending the use of conventional monetary and fiscal policies to solve Japan's problems. There is a consensus among the papers that using fiscal policy to stimulate the economy is not an option because the government's deficit and outstanding liabilities are already so high.[17] There is also a consensus that,

---

[15] On financial *keiretsu*, see Aoki and Saxonhouse (2000).

[16] For an analysis of Japan's permanent employment practices that provides perspective on the community-banking business model, see Boberg (2000).

[17] As noted, Kuttner and Posen (2001) and Ahearne et al. (2002) do not share this view. In January 2003, Prime Minister Koizumi abandoned his long-standing opposition to using fiscal policy to stimulate the economy and abandoned his pledge to cap new government bond issues for the fiscal year 2000 at 30 trillion yen (*Nihon keizai shimbun*, 31 January, 2003).

whatever the causes, Japan is facing a liquidity trap, and that conventional monetary policy will not restore Japan's economic health.

a. Exchange Rate Stability

If conventional fiscal and monetary policies will not work, what policies are recommended? Goyal and McKinnon see Japan mired in a low-interest rate liquidity trap because of a negative risk premium. The negative risk premium arises from: (1) decades of accumulation of dollar assets within Japanese financial institutions; and (2) fluctuations in the yen/dollar exchange rate, which increase the risks to yen-based firms from holding these dollar assets. Because running trade deficits cannot suddenly reverse the cumulative effect of decades of trade surpluses, according to Goyal and McKinnon, the only immediate policy instrument available for reducing the foreign exchange risk in Japanese financial intermediaries is to stabilise the yen/dollar exchange rate in a completely convincing fashion.[18] With the full cooperation of the United States, such a policy could be successful. With the end of the negative risk premium, nominal interest rates would rise, permitting the BOJ to once again use monetary policy to re-inflate the economy, while also restoring the profitability of bank lending.

b. Changing Price Expectations

Goyal and McKinnon view a rise in the nominal interest rate as a precondition for making effective use of monetary policy. In contrast, Ito and Fukao believe that monetary policy can be effective, even at a nominal interest rate of zero, provided the BOJ sets a credible inflation target of zero to three per cent.[19]

How such credibility might be achieved in the midst of deflationary conditions is rather uncertain. Five different channels that might achieve this end have been suggested. These channels include: (1) monetising the Japanese government debt; (2) the purchase by the MOF and the BOJ of privately-held non-governmental domestic financial and non-financial assets;[20] (3) the purchase by the BOJ of foreign financial assets;[21] (4) manipulation of the consumption tax; and (5) introduction of time-limited scrip and currency taxes.

---

[18] How this might be done is laid on in more detail in McKinnon and Ohno (2001).

[19] The magnitude of the target will depend on what is assumed about Japan's full employment real interest rate.

[20] In a more limited way than discussed here, the BOJ has already purchased some commercial paper, corporate bonds, and asset-back securities under repurchase agreements. These purchases have all been made from financial institutions. Thus far, none have been made in the open market or directly from corporations. See *Nihon keizai shimbun* (17 March, 2003).

[21] While the MOF has direct jurisdiction over foreign exchange trading, monthly purchases of 200–300 billion yen in foreign bonds are within the BOJ authority. See *Nihon keizai shimbun* (18 February, 2002).

None of these channels can work without the public perception that a long-term shift in government policy has taken place. If the BOJ intervention in private assets markets in Japan (for equities, corporate bonds, land, golf club memberships, woodblock prints, ceramics, or National Treasures and the like) or in foreign assets markets abroad is seen as temporary, in a deflationary environment, the supply of most such assets at the current price is likely to be highly elastic, making significant increases in Japanese prices, or a significant depreciation of the yen, much more difficult.[22]

(i) Printing money

Monetising the Japanese government debt (the direct purchase of newly issued public bonds by the BOJ) has been much discussed in recent years in Japan. Under intense political pressure from elements in the Liberal Democratic Party, the BOJ has begun to buy long-term government bonds from the public, as well as from banks, but it has not yet purchased any such bond than has been issued more recently than one year. The BOJ has resisted buying new issues on the grounds that this would lead to the perception of fiscal indiscipline.

Ihori et al. surmise that concern about the size of Japan's public debt weakens the private sector's incentive to spend.[23] This suggests that the real issue may be less whether or not the BOJ is buying new bond issues, but rather what it does with a bond issue after its purchase. If Ihori et al. are correct, and if it is the size of gross public debt and not only net public debt that is a matter of concern, then if the BOJ undertakes some polite equivalent of burning government bonds, deficit financing can proceed, in principle, without Japan's fiscal position becoming unsustainable.[24]

Historically a government will monetise its debt when investors do not have enough confidence that the government will honour its debts and are reluctant to buy its bonds. This has not been a problem that Japan has faced to date. Quite the contrary. Monetising the debt means that a government is getting its fiscal house in order not by cutting expenditures or increasing taxes, but rather by printing money. In the tradition of prudent central banking, the BOJ fears that an overt move to allow government expenditures to be made without the constraint of having to raise revenues through taxes or bonds will lead to such a dramatic change in price expectations that the bond market may suffer a severe decline. Fukao voices concern about this possibility in his paper. Japanese government bonds form an important part of the balance sheet of almost all Japanese financial

---

[22] For a discussion of how yen depreciation can promote Japanese economy recovery, see Svensson (2001).

[23] For a contrary view, once again see Kuttner and Posen (2001) and Ahearne et al. (2002).

[24] On the difference between Japan's net and gross public debt, see OECD (2000, p. 65). On monetising a portion of the Japanese debt, see Bernanke (2000, p. 163).

institutions. A severe decline in the bond market would destroy what equity remains in the banking system. As Fukao notes, the very change in price expectations that he seeks that would allow higher rates on loans permitting banks to once again operate profitably might be self-defeating. From this perspective, the Japanese economy is on a knife-edge. Because of the size of the public debt, the Japanese public, concerned that in the future the government will have either to cut back on entitlements or raise taxes, is reluctant to spend. Yet, if the government opts for a third way and prints money, the public might be altogether too ready to spend and more inflation than is desired might ensue.

The problem that Fukao identifies is similar to that faced by the US banking system after World War II. US banks in 1945 were flush with deposits, a disproportionate amount of which was invested in US government obligations. At the time there was concern that if bond prices fell by 20 per cent, the entire banking system could become insolvent. To guard against this possibility, the Federal Reserve System under the influence of the US Treasury supported the US government bond market agreeing to buy back government bonds at no less than par value, notwithstanding the inflationary consequences.[25] Only after the famous Accord of 1951 between these two government agencies was the Federal Reserve System once again free to pursue a contra-cyclical monetary policy.[26] Since March 2001, the BOJ has attempted to set what is tantamount to an inflation target at the lower bound (zero) of the range that Fukao and Ito propose.[27] The US experience of the late 1940s suggests that, in addition to the BOJ Policy Board's pledge to maintain interest rates at zero until deflation is ended, some pledge about supporting the bond market even after that target is achieved may be in order.

(ii) Manipulating the consumption tax

Monetary policy is not the only way to change price expectations. Both Ito and Ihori et al. note the important impact that the increase in Japan's consumption tax from three to five per cent in April 1997 had on Japan's recovery. During the year-and-a-half before Japan increased its consumption tax, the economy expanded faster than that of any other OECD country. During the quarter before the consumption-tax increase, Japan experienced a rate of GDP growth, a rate of growth of consumption expenditures, and a rate of growth of business investment all unmatched throughout the entire post-*bubble* period. This expansion came at a cost of later growth. Unlike Ito, Ihori et al. hold that, while the timing of this tightening of fiscal policy was unfortunate in view of the financial crisis that occurred in Asia that summer together with the collapse of two major financial

---

[25] See Samuelson (1948, pp. 354–55).
[26] See Samuelson (1961, p. 397).
[27] For a discussion of this, see Saxonhouse (2003).

institutions later that year, the negative impact of this policy was short-lived and cannot be held responsible for aborting Japan's recovery from the Lost Decade.

Ihori et al.'s perspective has led to proposals that Japan might temporarily lower the consumption tax to stimulate spending combined with a pre-announced increase well above five per cent in the future.[28] Alternatively, it has been suggested that inflationary expectations might be legislated by having Japan's Diet agree to a staggered set of pre-announced consumption-tax increases over a five-year period.[29] These proposals combine an unusually credible set of inflation targets with measures that attempt to resolve Japan's fiscal crisis. The deflationary impact of higher taxes would be more than offset here in the short-run by increased private spending. To the extent that Ihori et al. are correct and concerns over the sustainability of Japan's fiscal situation is affecting consumer spending, the resolution of this problem may soften the longer-run impact on consumer spending of higher taxes. Even if it does not, with price expectations reversed, monetary policy is once again free to play a role in stabilisation policy.

(iii) Taxing currency

Changing price expectations is needed as a means of lowering the real interest rate when it is assumed that the nominal interest rate cannot be pushed below zero. There are policies, however, that can push the nominal interest rate below zero, and by doing so remove the burden of creating inflationary expectations in a deflationary environment. Nominal interest rates are conventionally assumed not to be able to go below zero because no lender will accept a return less than zero when the option of holding currency at zero cost is available. But suppose that currency is taxed by the government so that the cost of holding it rises above zero. In this event, it does become possible for the nominal interest rate to fall below zero.[30] Happily, taxing currency has some of the same advantages as raising the consumption tax in that it promotes increased spending even while it helps to resolve Japan's fiscal problems.

One means of implicitly taxing currency is to have it lose its value in a pre-arranged periodic fashion following its issue. An extreme version of this might be government-issued scrip that has value only for a fixed period of time. Under pressure from Komeitō, a junior member of the three-party ruling coalition, Japan conducted a limited experiment with such a programme in 1999 by issuing scrip to families with children and to the elderly. This scrip retained its value for six months. The experiment, while extremely interesting, has not been repeated.[31]

---

[28] See Suzuki (2000) and Feldstein (2001).
[29] See Saxonhouse (1999) and Yasuba (2002). Vogelsgang (1999) recommends a cut in the consumption tax to zero and a staggered increase back to its original level.
[30] How this might be done is discussed in Buiter and Panigistzoglou (1999).
[31] For details and an evaluation of this programme, see Shimizutani (2002).

(iv) More reform of the financial system

In contrast to suggestions made that Japanese economic recovery can be promoted by reforming international financial arrangements and by the adoption of unconventional monetary and fiscal policies, Fukao and Nishimura and Kawamoto offer proposals to alter Japan's economic structure. Fukao wishes to promote competition in the financial services market by removing the public subsidies given to government-sponsored financial institutions. Unlike the usual situation, in this case, Fukao believes that promoting competition will raise rather than lower the price of financial services. This price increase, by allowing firms in the financial services sector that do not receive subsidies to operate profitably, will enhance rather than detract from national welfare.

Even while Fukao, like Prime Minister Koizumi, is effectively recommending privatising government-sponsored financial institutions, Nishimura and Kawamoto are recommending the creation of new ones. While believing that the range of community-banking practices should be circumscribed, Nishimura and Kawamoto mention that a place remains for such activities. They suggest that banks that retain this objective as their primary focus should be transformed into quasi-non-profit community organisations. The remaining firms in the banking sector would be expected to operate in such a way as to maximise shareholder value. In the current environment with so many borrowers whose credit is so poor, this should mean a substantial increase in the interest rates charged on many loans to reflect the risk involved in making them. Like Goyal and McKinnon and Fukao, Nishimura and Kawamoto believe that the key to the renewed health of the banking system is a greater spread between the interest charged on loans and the interest paid on deposits. But unlike Goyal and McKinnon and Fukao, Nishimura and Kawamoto see a structural change in the way that banks operate as the key to achieving this.

(v) Other supply-side changes

The structural, or supply-side problems, facing the Japanese economy are not confined to banking. To cite just one additional area among many others, just as the critical channel of credit creation and capital allocation cannot be restored to health without a change in the Government's relationship to this sector and a change in the governance of banks, so changes in educational and social security policies and a broader change in corporate governance must occur if Japanese economic recovery is going to be facilitated by a more efficient training and allocation of labour.[32] Inevitably as Fukao emphasises, the recovery of the Japanese economy will mix different strands of demand-side and supply-side changes.[33]

---

[32] For additional discussion of structural changes ongoing in the Japanese economy, see Saxonhouse (1998).

[33] Hayashi and Prescott (2002) stress the primary role of exogenous supply shocks in explaining Japan's performance in the 1990s.

5. CONCLUSIONS ON JAPAN'S LOST DECADE

There was nothing inevitable about the late 1980s *bubble* in Japan. The policy instruments available to the BOJ and the MOF could have averted it. At the same time, given the unusual circumstances in which *the bubble* developed, it is hardly surprising that Japan acted as it did. As in the United States in the late 1990s, during Japan's *bubble*, asset prices skyrocketed even while all conventional indicators that govern central bank policy such as the consumer price index, the wholesale price index, and the producer price index remained stable.

Once *the bubble* collapsed, however, neither the BOJ nor the MOF was quick to reverse policy to fight off the recession that ensued. The evidence presented at this Symposium suggests looser fiscal policy would have been ineffective. On the other hand, with prices still rising in the early 1990s and with short-term interest rates still above three per cent, Japan had not yet fallen into a liquidity trap. Monetary easing, if pursued aggressively, might have been successful. As it was, the BOJ, in error, kept the growth rate of base money extremely low through-out 1991–93.[34]

Japan, for whatever reason, having missed the opportunity to use monetary policy in the early 1990s, faced the last half of the 1990s, as today, unable to use the conventional tools of stabilisation policy to help it to recover. This does not mean that Japan was then, or is now, helpless. As noted, there is a large menu of unconventional fiscal measures, non-standard BOJ (and MOF) market interventions, corporate governance measures, and structural changes in the financial services sector that can help to rescue Japan. What remains discouraging after all these years is the absence of political will to adopt the kind of bold measures that can bring an end to the Lost Decade that goes on and on and on.

REFERENCES

Ahearne, A. et al. (2002), 'Preventing Deflation: Lessons from Japan's Experience in the 1990s', Board of Governors of the Federal Reserve System, International Finance Discussion Paper, No. 729 (June).

Ando, A. (2002), 'The Elusive Total Budget Outlay of the Japanese Government: An Inquiry into the Japanese National Accounts', *Journal of the Japanese and International Economics*, **16**, 177–93.

Aoki, M. and G. Saxonhouse (eds.) (2000), *Finance, Governance and Competitiveness in Japan* (Oxford: Oxford University Press).

Bergsten, C. F. (1988), *America in the World Economy: A Strategy for the 1990s* (Washington, DC: Institute for International Economics).

Bernanke, B. S. (2000), 'Japanese Monetary Policy: A Case of Self-Induced Paralysis?' in R. Mikitani and A. S. Posen (eds.), *Japan's Financial Crisis and Its Parallels to U.S. Experience* (Washington, DC: Institute for International Economics).

---

[34] For details, see Montgomery (2000).

Boberg, P. (2000), *Internal Labor Markets in Japanese Firms* (University of Michigan Department of Economics Doctoral Dissertation).

Buiter, W. H. and N. Panigistzoglou (1999), 'Liquidity Traps: How to Avoid Them and How to Escape Them,' National Bureau of Economic Research Working Paper No. 7245 (July).

Feldstein, M. (2001), 'Japan Needs to Stimulate Spending,' *Wall Street Journal* (16 July).

Frankel, J. A. (1991), 'Japanese Finance in the 1980s: A Survey', in P. Krugman (ed.), *Trade with Japan: Has the Door Opened Wider?* (Chicago: University of Chicago Press for NBER).

Hale, D. (1989), 'Tokyo to the Rescue', *Far Eastern Economic Review* (24 August), 60–61.

Hayashi, F. and E. C. Prescott (2002), 'The 1990s in Japan: A Lost Decade', *Review of Economic Dynamics*, **5**, 206–35.

Hubbard, R. G. (2002), 'Impediments to Growth in Japan' (Speech before the Japan Information Access Project Symposium, Washington, DC, 8 April).

Johnson, C. (1989), 'Their Behavior, Our Policy', *The National Interest*, **17**, 17–27.

Johnson, C. (1998), 'Economic Crisis in East Asia: The Clash of Capitalism', *Cambridge Journal of Economics*, **22**, 653–62.

Krugman, P. (1998), 'It's Baack: Japan's Slump and the Return of the Liquidity Trap', *Brookings Papers in Economic Activity*, 137–87.

Kuttner, K. N. and A. S. Posen (2001), 'The Great Recession: Lessons for Macroeconomic Policy from Japan', *Brookings Papers in Economic Activity*, 93–185.

McKinnon, R. and K. Ohno (1997), *Dollar and Yen: Resolving Economic Conflict between the United States and Japan* (Cambridge, MA: MIT Press).

McKinnon, R. and K. Ohno (2001), 'The Foreign Exchange Origins of Japan's Economic Slump and Low Interest Liquidity Trap', *The World Economy*, **24**, 279–317.

Montgomery, H. (2000), 'The Role of Regulatory Capital and Bank Credit in the Economy of Japan' (University of Michigan, Department of Economics Doctoral Dissertation).

Nihon, sorifu (1995), Nihon tōkeinenkan Heisei rokunen (1995).

Organization for Economic Co-operation and Development (OECD) (2000), *Economy Survey: Japan, 1999–2000* (Paris).

Ramaswamy, R. and C. Rendu (2000), 'Japan's Stagnant Nineties: A Vector Auto-Regressive Retrospective,' *IMF Staff Papers*, **47**, 259–78.

Samuelson, P. A. (1948), *Economics: An Introductory Analysis* (1st ed., New York: McGraw Hill).

Samuelson, P. A. (1961), *Economics: An Introductory Analysis* (5th ed., New York: McGraw Hill).

Saxonhouse, G. R. (1998), 'Structural Change and Japanese Economic History: Will the 21st Century be Different?' *American Economic Review*, **88**, 408–11.

Saxonhouse, G. R. (1999), 'Japan's Growth Conundrum', *Financial Times* (14 June).

Saxonhouse, G. R. (2003), 'Prospective Japanese Economic Recovery: Perspectives from European Economic Recovery in the 1930s', in Stern (2003).

Shimizutani, S. (2002), 'Consumption and Tax Policy in Japan in the 1990s: Evidence from House-hold Data' (University of Michigan, Department of Economics Doctoral Dissertation).

Sims, C. A. (1980), 'Macroeconomics and Reality', *Econometrica*, **48**, 1–48.

Stern, R. M. (ed.) (2003), *Japan's Economic Recovery: Commercial Policy, Monetary Policy, and Corporate Governance* (Cheltenham, UK: Edward Elgar, forthcoming).

Suzuki, Y. (2000), 'Strategies for Overcoming Japan's Economic Crisis', in M. Aoki and G. R. Saxonhouse (eds.), *Finance, Governance and Competitiveness in Japan* (Oxford: Oxford University Press).

Svensson, L. E. O. (2001), 'The Zero-Bound in an Open Economy: A Fool-Proof Way of Escaping the Liquidity Trap', *Monetary and Economic Studies*, **19**, 277–321.

Vogelsgang, M. (1999), 'How to Rescue Japan: Proposal of a Staggered VAT Reform', University of Potsdam, European Institute for International Economic Relations, Discussion Paper, No. 61 (May).

Walker, W. C. (2002), 'Ricardian Equivalence and Fiscal Policy Effectiveness in Japan', *Asian Economic Journal*, **16**, 285–302.

Werner, R. A. (2002), 'Monetary Policy Implementation in Japan: What They Say versus What They Do', *Asian Economic Journal* (forthcoming).

Yasuba, Y. (2002) *Asahi Shimbun* (27 March).

2

Retrospective on the Bubble Period and its Relationship to Developments in the 1990s

Takatoshi Ito

1. INTRODUCTION

THE Japanese economy has experienced a boom and bust in the last twenty years. The economic boom, accompanied by land and stock price increases, in the 1980s was followed by the stagnant, low growth period, accompanied by the declines in land and stock prices. The boom is now known as *the bubble period*, and the stagnation is now known as *the lost decade*.

Stock prices rose three-fold from the end of 1985 to 1989 and then lost all that gain in the following twelve years, with most of the decline in the first two and a half years. The Nikkei 225 stock index was 13,000 at the end of 1985. It rose three-fold in the next four years, and reached about 39,000 – to be precise, 38,916 on the last trading day of 1989. Then stock prices lost more than 60 per cent in the next two and a half years. Stock prices fluctuated in the following ten years, but hit a post-bubble low of 11,819.70 – less than a third of the peak – on 13 March, 2001. The current level of the stock price index is where it was 16 years ago.[1]

The story is the same, or even worse, for land prices. Land prices increased three-fold from 1985 to 1990 and declined to the same level by 2000. The average land price index for the six largest metropolitan areas stood at 35.1 in

TAKATOSHI ITO is from the University of Tokyo. He would like to thank Ted Truman, Robert Barsky, and other Symposium participants for helpful comments.

[1] The composition of the Nikkei 225 index was changed in April 2000. According to some analysts' calculations, the Nikkei under the old composition is about 4,000 points higher than the old Nikkei at the present time.

September 1985 (with March 1990 = 100), and it rose to 105.1 in September 1990. That is, a three-fold increase in five years. Then the land price index gradually declined over the following ten years. The index in September 2000 was 34.6, below its level and is still dropping.

The bursting of the bubble created the well-known balance-sheet problems for many banks and corporations and contributed to the stagnant decade of the 1990s, which is now commonly known as '*the lost decade.*' Since weak economic activities were accompanied by financial crises that were a result of the burst bubble, *the bubble* itself is often blamed as the origin of *the lost decade*.

Three large banks failed in 1997–98, and many other smaller banks have failed since 1995. The banking sector presently is still not healthy, and mergers among large banks, which became popular in 2001–02, do not seem to have produced healthier banks. The average GDP growth rate from 1991 to 2000 was less than 1.5 per cent. This is shockingly low compared to the average of four per cent growth from 1975 to 1990. Even after ten years since the burst bubble became obvious, the Japanese economy has not recovered. For three consecutive quarters starting from the second quarter of 2001, the GDP growth rate has been negative. Prices have been decreasing for the last three years. A deflationary spiral – deflation causes an increased debt burden, which affects consumption and investment, which in turn lowers aggregate demand, thus aggravating deflation – seems to have set in. With the nominal interest rate equal to zero and the debt to GDP ratio being extremely high (140 per cent), the scope for conventional monetary and fiscal policy stimulus is quite limited. How could Japan fall into such a mess?

With the benefit of hindsight, this paper will investigate three questions: (1) how big was *the bubble*, and what caused it? (2) could, and should, policy measures have prevented (most of) *the bubble*? (3) what was the contribution of *the bubble* to *the lost decade*?

In the literature, there have been many studies of the asset-price inflation and deflation in Japan. The conventional wisdom concerning these questions is as follows. (1) Too loose monetary policy for too long produced *the bubble*. Monetary policy was in error. (2) An early tightening would have prevented (most of) *the bubble*. It would have been better to prevent *the bubble* from forming or expanding. (3) *The bubble* and its bursting made the financial system unstable in the 1990s and thus contributed to *the lost decade*.

In what follows, I will propose a slight revision to the conventional wisdom. (1) *The bubble* was only part of a surge in economic activities. (2) It would have been neither possible nor desirable to employ monetary policy to achieve asset-price stabilisation. Supervision policy, rather than monetary policy, should have been employed aggressively. (3) *The lost decade* is a result of the burst bubble and policy mistakes, with an increasing weight on the latter over time.

2. THE BUBBLE AND THE LOST DECADE

Asset prices started to increase in the mid-1980s. In the beginning, the increases in stock and land prices were considered to be a result of good fundamentals. Indeed, the economy was growing at a rate exceeding four per cent, and accelerating toward the end of the 1980s. The stock prices and land prices started to rise sharply at around 1984, and continued their increase toward the 1990s. The consumer price inflation stayed moderate until 1988. Even in 1989, when the prices started to rise, the inflation rate was below three per cent. Accelerating economic growth with moderate inflation, accompanied by rising asset prices, looked great at the time.

The peak of the stock prices turned out to be the last trading day of 1989, when the Nikkei 225 index reached a level just shy of 40,000 yen. The stock prices quickly lost ground in 1990, and again in 1992. By the summer of 1992, the level of the stock prices was below 16,000 yen, 40 per cent of the peak. The economic growth rate in 1990 was above four per cent, and it was still at three per cent in 1991. In 1992, the economic growth rate came down to below one per cent. It became clear by mid-1992 that the best time had passed. However, many expected, or hoped, that the drop in asset prices was a correction of the excess and prices would not drop further. Not very many had predicted that the stock and land prices would continue to slide in the following ten years.

The bubble and its collapse can be viewed in the mountain shape of stock and land price levels from 1980 to 2001 as shown in Figure 1. A first question is how

FIGURE 1
Japanese Stock and Land Price Index, 1980–2001

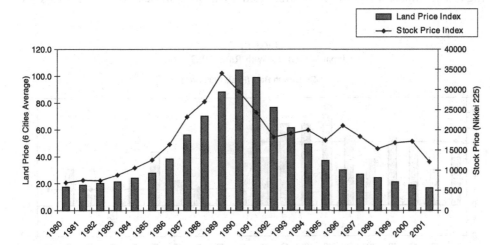

Notes:
The land price index refers to commercial land in six metropolitan cities in September of each year, as calculated by the Real Estate Institute. The Stock Price Index is the Nikkei 225, Annual average of daily close, as provided by the Nihon Keizai Shinbun.

much of this mountain was a bubble. Looking at the level of land prices, the level
in 2001 is where it was in 1980. Stock prices dipped below 10,000 yen in the
aftermath of September 11th. The 10,000 mark was the level at the end of 1983.
Should we regard the rise and fall of stock prices from 1983 to 2001 as a result
of speculative activities?

The economy remained stagnant from 1992 to 1995. Stock prices recovered
somewhat and fluctuated between 17,000 and 20,000 for most of the four years.
Land prices continued a gradual descent. The period from the autumn of 1995 to
the first quarter of 1997 was one of recovery. However, the fragile recovery was
quickly aborted in a series of events in 1997. In April 1997, the consumption tax
rate and social securities contribution rate were increased, and the special tax cut
of the preceding two years was repealed. The temporary decrease in spending
from these measures was compounded by the deflationary impact of the Asian
currency crisis that started in Thailand in July 1997 and spread to the rest of Asia
by the end of the year and by the financial crisis in Japan in November 1997.
The deflationary impact of these events hit the Japanese economy hard, and the
growth rate in 1998 was negative for the first time since 1974.

When the growth rate is plotted from 1982 to 2001 in Figure 2, there is a clear
break at around 1991–92. The average growth rate of the 1980s was four per
cent, and for the ten years since 1992, one per cent. Why is the growth rate of
the 1990s so much lower than that of the 1980s? Was it necessary to experience
the lower growth rate in the burst bubble period?

The asset-price declines caused non-performing loans to increase, as more
construction companies and real estate companies stopped repaying their borrowings. The financial institutions first tried to absorb losses from bad loans by

FIGURE 2
Japan's GDP Growth Rate, 1982–2001

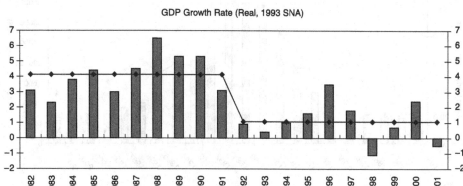

Notes:
Calculated from Government of Japan, System of National Accounts (SNA).

postponing resolution of the bad-loan problem. The typical example was the *jusen* problem (housing loan companies that were liquidated in 1995, after several years of indecision), detailed in Cargill et al. (1997, Ch. 6). When problems spread to larger banks from the *jusen*, again the regulators and politicians did not take early, pre-emptive action. There was no legal structure to close insolvent banks, or inject capital into weak banks. It was only after the crisis of November 1997 – in which two securities firms and one large bank failed – that the government prepared funds for capital injection. In 1998, two more large banks failed. Capital injections in 1998 and 1999 seemingly restored the health of major banks. (See Cargill et al., 2000, for these developments.) IT stock prices soared from the autumn of 1999 to the spring of 2000, raising hope for economic recovery, led by increasing asset prices. Indeed, the growth rate in 2000 exceeded two per cent. However, the economy plunged into a recession again in 2001.

As economic activity considerably slowed down after 1997, the general price levels started to decline. When the effect of the consumption tax rate increase in April 1997 is removed, the CPI inflation rate has been virtually zero from 1995 to 1998 and has become negative since 1999. From 2001–02, the inflation rate is about negative one per cent. The deflation problem is serious, as the nominal interest rate cannot be negative. The real interest rate remains positive, as long as the inflation rate is negative. The unemployment rate rose sharply, by Japanese standards, after 1998 to exceed five per cent. The movement of prices and unemployment rate, as shown in Figure 3, raise a serious concern for the prospect of the Japanese economy, in 2002 and beyond.

FIGURE 3
Inflation and Unemployment, 1980–2001

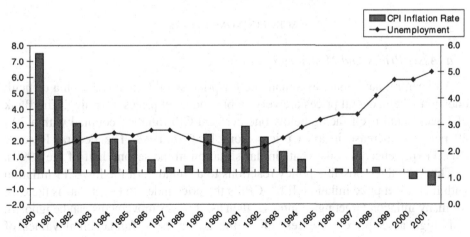

Source: See Figure 2.

In sum, there were several signs of recovery in the 1990s, but in each case, the recovery fizzled in a few quarters. After *the lost decade*, the position of the Japanese economy is no better than immediately after the burst bubble. In fact, in several ways, the situation in 2002 is worse than it was in 1992. The interest rate has been lowered to zero, but the inflation rate remains negative. Thus the real interest rate remains relatively high for the stagnant economy. The debt-GDP ratio became the highest among the G7 nations as the result of several fiscal stimulus packages, and the sustainability of the fiscal debt is now seriously questioned by credit rating agencies. Banks are still under growing burdens of non-performing loans. Three years after the 1999 capital injections, banks have again depleted their own capital and the market regards many of them to be either insolvent or too weak to survive. What could be appropriate policy options at this point is a challenging and important question, but that is not the theme of this paper. (See, for example, Ito, 2001, for a possible solution for this problem.)

The current difficulties of the Japanese economy are a result of several factors. The bubble of the 1980s is of course responsible for the burst bubble problem of 1992–1995. But, how much of the lost decade problem is due to the burst bubble problem? If the regulators had taken appropriate action to nip the non-performing loans problem in the bud, the banking crisis of 1997 might not have occurred. Several policy mistakes were committed. Monetary policy remained too tight for too long in the 1990s, and the fiscal tightening of April 1997 may have aborted the fragile recovery at the time.

Of course, it is difficult to separate the contributions of each factor toward the lost decade. But, not all of the problems can be traced back to the bubble problem. Let us now review what caused *the bubble*, and come back to the question of what caused *the lost decade*.

3. MACROECONOMIC ASPECTS

a. Asset Prices and Monetary Policy

Any central bank that has a mandate for price stability is faced with a difficult question when general prices are very stable and asset prices are rising. The Bank of Japan found itself facing below one per cent CPI inflation coupled with a 30–40 per cent increase in asset prices from 1986 to 1988. The Federal Reserve Board experienced a somewhat similar situation in the second half of the 1990s.

There are three possible policy reactions to a situation of the low-CPI inflation with high-asset price inflation. If the CPI is the price index to target – as is the case for many inflation targeting countries – then asset prices movements can be ignored.

If high asset price increases reflect the advances in fundamental values of assets – say, as in the 'new' economy – then that should be welcomed and not be a matter of concern. However, if the asset price increases are the result of a bubble, then monetary policy possibly has some role to prevent the bubble from over-expanding, because the burst bubble would certainly cause painful adjustments to the economy. The problem is that it is difficult to distinguish asset price increases due to 'fundamental' reasons and those due to a bubble.

Ito and Iwaisako (1996) examined the issue of whether the asset price increases could be justified by the simple asset pricing model, or be better viewed as a stochastic bubble process. When the interest rate is lowered and the expected growth rate increases, it is natural that the ratio of asset prices to dividends will increase. With appropriate assumptions, the price-dividend ratio (P/D) can be taken to be proportional to the difference between the interest rate and the growth (of dividend) ratio:

$$P/D = 1/(r - g).$$

Suppose that the interest rate is lowered from six to five per cent and the growth rate rises from three to four per cent, then the blow-up factor (P/D) goes from 33.3 to 100, that is a three-fold increase. This was the approximate change in Japanese stock prices from 1985 to 1989. This logic was used in several studies in an attempt to justify the spectacular rise in asset prices. (Ueda, 1990, stood out in questioning the logic behind the stock-price increases before stock prices started to decline.) Ito and Iwaisako (1996) showed that the logic was flawed, because the change in the interest rate could not be regarded as a permanent event. Depending on how long the low interest rate would last, the blow-up factor of the price/yield ratio would not rise much. If the interest rate was cut from six to five per cent and the growth rate increased from three to four per cent for only three years, instead of permanently, the blow-up factor is only six per cent, instead of 200 per cent. (See Ito and Iwaisako, 1996, reproduced in Cargill et al., 1997.)

It is easy to characterise the second half of the 1980s as a bubble period, but it is difficult to model it theoretically. A rational bubble (and a Ponzi game) tends to exist forever and never crash. If it is known that a bubble will burst in the future, it may not occur at all. A stochastic bubble model is capable of producing the bursting of a bubble. Ito and Iwaisako (1996) simulated a stochastic bubble model, and showed that the actual path of stock prices from 1985 to 1994 can be simulated as a combination of two stochastic bubbles. However, the model does not explain why it started in the first place, and how the probability of burst bubbles can be determined. Their conclusion is that the first part of asset price movements may be regarded as reactions to a favourable economic environment (fundamentals) in the first half of the 1980s, while stochastic bubbles were added to price increases due to fundamentals in the second half of the 1980s. It was hard to distinguish how much can be attributable to fundamentals and how much to bubbles at the time of the price increases.

An advocate of a central bank as a CPI-only targeter (disregarding asset prices) would argue as follows. If asset prices are increasing due to fundamental reasons (such as higher demand) without provoking general price increases, then the central bank with a general price-stability mandate should not tighten. If asset prices are increasing due to a bubble, the central bank may not tighten either, so long as it does not affect the CPI. This is because asset prices go up and down and some people make money and some lose. But it is not the role of the central bank to intervene in income transfers with voluntary participation. A hardline advocate of this position might go further to argue that housing-related prices should not be included in the CPI. A non-hardliner would argue that the CPI should include housing-related expenses (rents and imputed rents or mortgage payment costs), and monetary policy should pay attention to asset prices within the bound of their influences on the CPI.

Even when one takes a position that the central bank should target CPI inflation only, asset prices are useful if they play a role as a leading indicator. The forward-looking inflation targeter can tighten even with a low CPI, if convinced of impending CPI inflation using all the information available including asset price information. The difficulty with this argument is that the lag between asset price increases and CPI increases may be uncertain. If productivity increases are causing asset prices to increase, it may be a long time before this spills over to general price levels. Even in the case of a bubble causing asset price inflation, the duration of a bubble is extremely uncertain.

There could be another position that takes asset prices a little more seriously. Asset prices may be a part of the cost of living, beyond just rents and imputed rents. An increase in asset prices then requires tightening just like any other prices. Therefore, even in the absence of inflation of the CPI, regularly defined, monetary policy could turn to tightening. There are two ways to incorporate the asset price as a leading indicator in monetary-policy considerations. One way is to modify the price indicators that the central bank would target so that asset prices – stock prices and housing prices – would have more weight in the new price indicator. Another way is that the central bank decides to target both inflation indicators, CPI, regularly defined, and some asset-price index – say the combination of stock and real estate prices. The difficulty of this position is that there is no theory or enough case experience to help choose the right weights on asset prices for targeting price stability.

The third position is a more eclectic one. The central bank can pay serious attention to asset price inflation, because a cycle of forming a bubble and bursting it would adversely affect the economy. The damage may come from the real-estate side. Over-investment that leads to a prolonged recession while first drawing workers into sectors that are bound to shrink later results in very serious mis-allocations of resources. The damage could also come from the financial side. The bursting of a bubble most likely damages the balance sheets of financial institutions because borrowers, including many real estate and construction companies, cannot repay the debt accumulated during the bubble. The insolvent and weak financial institutions pose systemic risks, not to mention causing a credit crunch. The eclectic position sounds sensible, considering what happened to Japan in the 1980s and 1990s. The Japanese economy is thus still struggling since the end of the lost decade that followed the bubble period.

The eclectic position is put forward in Cecchetti et al. (2000), which considers the question of how the central bank should respond to asset price movements, and Okina et al. (2001), which reviews the Bank of Japan policy during the 1980s. Cecchetti et al. (2000) recommend that the central bank should pay attention to asset prices by measuring the degree of mis-pricing in asset prices, but they do not recommend that the central bank intentionally kill the bubble. Okina et al. (2001) emphasise the danger of *the bubble* in their reflection on the Japanese experiences in the last two decades. Any gains in output or asset prices during *the bubble* seemed to be lost in the subsequent years, and many financial institutions were in trouble. In order to maintain financial stability, any unusual asset-price increases should be checked by the central bank. Okina et al. admit that there was an error in monetary policy and that too loose monetary policy was maintained too long. However, they also argue that the monetary-policy decision was influenced by the 'prevailing policy agenda,' which included policy coordination (1985–87) as a priority to stop yen appreciation and fiscal consolidation and bullish assessment in the government (1987–89). 'In 1989, the BOJ began seriously addressing the question of raising the official discount rate, but could not succeed in persuading the government or the general public on the need to tighten monetary policy' (Okina et al., 2001, p. 424).

Although it would be difficult to contradict what has been advocated in the eclectic position, there remain concerns about this approach. First, could the central bank measure the size of mis-pricing? As was shown in Japan and the United States, it is extremely difficult to measure the size of the bubble, if not its existence at all, when the economy is in the bubble. It becomes apparent that the bubble may have existed only after it was over. Second, wouldn't the central bank tend to kill the bubble prematurely or overkill it once it happens, according to the eclectic position? When Chairman Greenspan warned about the stock-price increases with his famous phrase, 'irrational exuberance,' the Dow was well below 10,000. Even after the IT bubble burst, the Dow remained for a long period at around 10,000 (with a sharp dip and recovery after September 11th). If Chairman Greenspan had acted on his own remark with a tightening of monetary policy, the long expansion of the economy might have been terminated prematurely.

In sum, there are three possible answers to the question of what the central bank should do when it sees rising asset prices without CPI inflation: (a) target CPI only; no attention to asset prices, except that they may be a leading indicator of future CPI inflation; (b) target price indicators with asset prices weighted higher than CPI; (c) eclectic. Primarily target the CPI but also watch asset prices, because a bubble and its bursting affects adversely the real and financial sides of the economy.

b. The Japanese Bubble in the 1980s

Spectacular economic growth combined with low inflation and rising asset prices happened in unique circumstances in the second half of the 1980s in Japan. The second half of the 1980s was characterised by several major events that were unprecedented. The rapid yen appreciation from 260 yen/dollar in February 1985 to 150 yen/dollar in the summer of 1986 was one of the most dramatic changes in the value of the yen. The process broke the then historical high of 178 yen/dollar. In October 1987, US stock prices declined sharply – Black Monday – setting off an alarm to the rest of the world. Against this background, the economic performance and asset price movements should be evaluated carefully.

Okina et al. (2001) analyse the mechanism for creating and expanding *the bubble*, the responsibility of Bank of Japan policy in that mechanism, and the reasons for the delayed tightening, before drawing lessons for future policy. Although their analysis of *the bubble* is quite sensible from an economic point of view, with the benefit of hindsight it does not give serious thought to how a central bank in the future may act in a period of asset-price inflation. So, let us undertake some counter-factual exercise to suggest at what point the Bank of Japan should have tightened the monetary policy and by how much.

The Bank of Japan cut the interest rate five times between 1986 and 1987:

30 January, 1986: 5 per cent → 4.5 per cent
10 March, 1986: 4.5 per cent → 4.0 per cent (at the same time with the Federal Reserve and Bundesbank)
21 April, 1986: 4.0 per cent → 3.5 per cent (with the Federal Reserve)
1 November, 1986: 3.5 per cent → 3.0 per cent (at the same time with the Miyazawa-Baker announcement on the exchange rate accord)
23 February, 1987: 3.0 per cent → 2.5 per cent (The Louvre Accord).

Then the rate was maintained until 31 May, 1989. Once the interest rate started to increase, it was raised very quickly:

31 May, 1989: 2.5 per cent → 4.25 per cent
11 October, 1989: 3.25 per cent → 3.75 per cent
25 December, 1989: 3.75 per cent → 4.25 per cent
20 March, 1990: 4.25 per cent → 5.25 per cent
30 August, 1990: 5.25 per cent → 6.0 per cent.

The decisions to lower interest rates in 1986 and 1987 are characterised by Okina et al. as being influenced by the priority given to international policy coordination in order to stop yen appreciation. Then, once the official discount rate was lowered to the then unprecedented low level of 2.5 per cent, the Bank of Japan could not find an opportune time to raise the rate until May 1989. Okina et al. seem to regret that the interest rate was too low in 1987 and was not raised earlier than May 1989.

It is possible to identify three possible decision points when the Bank of Japan might have taken different actions. Namely, the last discount-rate cut (23 February, 1987) in the series, from three to 2.5 per cent, was one too many. The official discount rate could have been raised in the summer of 1987. Failing that, the official discount rate could have been raised in August 1988, when the Federal Reserve and Bundesbank raised interest rates. The last two opportunities being missed, the discount rate rise (31 May, 1989; 2.5 per cent → 3.25 per cent) was too late.

Among these three counter-factual possibilities, raising the interest rate in 1988 is the most realistic. Stock prices in Japan recovered from the pre-Black Monday peak earlier than Germany or the United States, and there was scope to raise the interest rate at the time the other countries raised the interest rate. However, by the summer of 1988, stock and land prices had risen considerably. Nipping the last run of *the bubble* from 1988 to 1989 might have been helpful, but questions would remain. If further rise of the stock and land prices was an objective, how much should the interest rate have been raised in the summer of 1988?

There is yet another question about whether the central bank should consider asset prices because of the concern about financial stability after the burst bubble. This is that financial stability can be better monitored by supervision policy rather than monetary policy. Making the financial system more resistant to fluctuations in asset prices through supervision policy may be better than trying to limit fluctuations in asset prices by monetary policy.

4. MICROECONOMIC AND INSTITUTIONAL ASPECTS

a. Prudential Regulations

Prudential policies are the key to preventing excessive lending that is often at the heart of a bubble problem. It is often argued that banking supervision has long been based on a principle of the so-called convoy system, that is, no bank should fail and the speed of progress is set with the slowest. It is believed that as entry and competition are restricted, the industry will remain healthy. At least in retrospect, when the regulatory regime was shifted to allow more competition in the mid-1980s, the supervision regime should have been enhanced in Japan.

In general, two types of prudential policies can be differentiated in their relationship to asset price inflation: (1) those that induce financial institutions to behave so that a bubble would not emerge in the first place; and (2) those that induce financial institutions to become resistant against asset price fluctuations. Some of the first type of prudential policies tend to be 'procyclical.'

One of the well-known supervision policies at the time of the Japanese *bubble* was the adoption of the Basle risk-based capital adequacy rule that was internationally agreed upon in 1988. The risk-based capital ratio was gradually raised during the transition period, and the rule was fully implemented in 1993. As is well known, this rule is now being reviewed by the Basle Committee on Banking Supervision, and many of the issues mentioned below are to be addressed in this exercise toward Basle II.

Without prejudicing what is being discussed in the Basle Committee, it is interesting to raise some theoretical questions related to this rule. For example, did the Basle capital adequacy rule act either to prevent emergence of the Japanese *bubble* or to make Japanese banks more resistant against a bubble and its burst?

My answer to the first question is as follows. The role of the Basle capital adequacy rule to prevent a bubble from emerging appears to have been limited. According to the 1988 rule, the risk weight of commercial lending is uniformly 100 per cent, regardless of the sector to which the lending is to be extended or whether the collateral is secured.

In theory, when a sharp increase of asset prices occurs, the future volatility of this asset price should be considered to be higher. Taking into account this increased risk, lending to real-estate-related sectors should be curtailed and the loan-value ratio should be lowered. This change in bank lending behaviour can be induced by a well-designed regulatory regime, an ad hoc direct regulation, or internal risk management of banks. But, none of this occurred in the second half of the 1980s. The lending to the real-estate sector increased in the second half of the 1980s, and the loan-value ratio did not decline but even rose. This put banks in a vulnerable position by the end of the 1980s.

Second, the Basle capital adequacy rule probably contributed to make Japanese banks more resistant against incurring losses by imposing a higher capital ratio than otherwise. However, there was one clause that had attracted a lot of attention. Japanese banks were allowed to count as Tier II capital 45 per cent of the latent capital gains from long-held stocks. Since Japanese banks held relatively large amounts of stocks, typically under cross-share holding arrangements, they benefited from this clause, as stock prices soared in 1988 and 1989. Then with the crash of the stock market in 1992 and 1993, Japanese banks had to issue subordinated debts to make up the loss in the Tier II capital due to the stock price declines. Many observers believe that the pressure from the capital adequacy ratio did not work when it was most needed (during *the bubble*) because the 45 per cent of latent capital gains was counted in.

As mentioned above, some prudential policy changes in response to a sharp increase in real estate and stock prices may have been desirable. Many believe that when asset prices were increasing sharply, prudential policies should have been designed differently so that the loan-value ratio would be lowered (either by direct regulation or preferably by some regulation to induce banks to do so), and that the share of lending to the real estate sector should be capped (again, by direct regulation or preferably by some regulation to induce banks to do so).

It was a little too late in terms of preventing a bubble, but the Ministry of Finance did introduce a blunt measure in April 1990. It asked banks not to increase the amount of total lending to the real-estate-related sector. This indeed capped bank lending and contributed to the end of land bubble. Although the stock bubble had ended three months earlier, it was not clear that land prices would not rise further. The measure was generally considered to have made sure that the real-estate bubble would end. It is an interesting counterfactual question whether this blunt measure should have been introduced two years earlier, and if so, whether it would have made a difference in the magnitude of *the bubble*.

What the Japanese authorities could have done in the second half of the 1980s includes the following: (1) introduce a regulation (or guidance) on the loan/value ratio on real estate lending, citing an increased risk in the real estate price volatility; and (2) issue a regulation (or guidelines) to limit lending to real-estate-related sectors, citing the risks of concentrating loans to a single sector. Regulation (1) is a type of regulation that the Hong Kong regulators imposed upon its banks during its bubble period. In fact, regulation (2) was issued in 1990, too late to prevent the Japanese bubble from expanding to a dangerous proportion.

b. Tax Issues

(i) Mortgage interest payment deductibility

Tax incentives may also contribute to asset-price inflation. In Japan, mortgage interest payments are not deductible from income. Incentives for Japanese home-owners are in the form of tax credits, but requirements on income, floor space, and other characteristics are rather strict. Basically, with bigger houses for high-income individuals, small mortgage takers are not able to take full advantage of the system, so it is unlikely that the tax credit system contributed to *the bubble*. Besides, it is inconceivable that the tax incentive for owner-occupied housing by itself would contribute to asset inflation (at least the bubble process), because the transaction costs of buying and selling owner-occupied housing are substantial, and not very many individuals speculate by moving around very often with owner-occupied housing. The incentive may increase the 'level' of housing prices, but there is no mechanism of tax saving for home ownership that would accelerate asset inflation. An effect of the tax system on a bubble process may be present for rental property, or second-home property, but not for owner-occupied housing.

(ii) Capital gains vs. dividend (or rent)

If dividend income is taxed at higher rates than capital gains, tax-induced behaviour can interact with expectations of future asset prices in a manner that would increase the amplitude of asset price movements (at least in the stock-price series not adjusted for dividends). It follows that a question can be raised as to whether the tax considerations discussed above contributed to the exaggeration of asset-price movements. That is: (a) if periods of misalignment had been preceded by actual or prospective changes in the tax system; (b) if policy reforms in other areas (financial markets) had inadvertently sharpened incentives embedded in existing tax arrangements; and (c) if there were any other destabilising factors that the tax system helped to amplify.

In Japan, realised capital gains on real estate have been taxed separately from other types of income for individuals. The highest rate was 32.5 per cent in 1988, and it was raised to 39 per cent in 1991 in order to curb speculative transactions. On the one hand, this was clearly too late, if the intended effect was to prevent a bubble. But, on the other hand, the timing coincided with the peak of *the bubble*. It is possible to argue that combined with the lending curb on banks, the higher rates for capital gains may have made certain the end of *the bubble*. Note that losses from real estate dealings could not be carried over, so that risks from investing in real estate were clearly high. Rents after expenses and amortisation had been usually taxed as regular income. It is not clear whether or not which rate is higher, as it depends on the income-tax brackets. For corporations, a special tax on short-term capital gains was introduced in 1987. So, at least for short-term gains, capital gains from land transactions were taxed much more heavily than rents. Therefore, with respect to real estate in Japan, the presumption that rents were taxed higher than real estate capital gains does not hold, possibly, except for very high income tax bracket individuals. Yet, there was a bubble.

(iii) Inheritance tax

One real-estate-related tax measure that is peculiar to Japan is the bequest tax. This tax may have contributed to the real estate bubble in Japan. (The inheritance tax is imposed on those who receive inheritance, while the estate tax in the United States is imposed on the estate of the deceased.) The process is as follows. The Japanese inheritance tax has a progressive marginal rate structure. Liabilities (mortgages) are fully deductible from the assessed property value, while the property is assessed, for inheritance tax purposes, at a substantial discount, and at even a deeper discount for the first 200 square metres of land).

Therefore, purchasing additional real estate (typically properties to rent out) with high leverage would create negative asset values for tax purposes, so that the positive values of other assets can be partially offset. During *the bubble* period in Japan, those who were planning a bequest to their heirs were alarmed as their real estate values went up. In order to avoid high taxes, they purchased more real estate with high leverage, so that they could lessen the bequest tax burden. The higher prices generated more demand for real estates due to tax distortions, and this could have created an upward spiral in prices.

This is theoretically true, and a well-known bequest strategy. Whether this bequest motive had a significant impact on the real estate market in general is uncertain, since as a total, individuals were net sellers during *the bubble* period, and corporations were net buyers.

(iv) Other taxes

The Japanese government introduced several tax measures to stem land price increases toward the end of *the bubble* period. Increasing land prices created a sense of widening inequality, and the government responded so that speculative activities could be stopped. The special cabinet-member group to deal with land prices was created as early as 1986. It was expanded in the following year, and then price monitoring for transactions was introduced. In 1987, differential land capital gains tax rates based on the holding period (longer or shorter than five years) were introduced. In addition, for corporations, a special tax category was introduced for a 'very short term' holding (less than two years). These changes were designed to discourage speculative activities (buying and selling in a short period). In 1988, the carryover of capital gains for owner-occupied housing was removed and replaced with a fixed deductibility (30 million yen) from capital gains of owner-occupied housing for more than ten years. Also in 1988, the bequest tax was changed so that any real estate acquired within three years of death should be evaluated at the purchase price, not the assessed price which was typically lower than the market price. In 1992, a new land tax was legislated. The land tax was imposed on holdings of large land lots in high-priced areas (30,000 yen per one square metre). In the three largest metropolitan areas, a special tax was designed to penalise holding of undeveloped land. In 1993, the special tax on holding unused land in the three metropolitan areas was revised so that parking lots were not exempted from tax and the minimum size for taxation was lowered to 1,000 square metres. After 1994, some of these measures have been reversed, as land prices continued to decline. These measures were meant to make transactions and holdings of land more expensive and making profits from trading real estate with short-term holding more difficult.

Did these changes in real-estate-related taxes have the intended effects? Most of the measures were introduced toward the end of *the bubble* period, so it was not a clean test for deciding whether these measures could have prevented a bubble. As the measures were introduced, the asset bubble was collapsing anyway. It might have put another nail in the coffin.

c. Securities

There was no capital gains tax on securities trading by individuals before 1988 unless individuals trade many times in a calendar year. After 1988, the choice was offered to individual investors. If a withholding tax method was selected, five per cent of the gross sales was presumed as capital gains and taxed at 20 per cent. Therefore, effectively, one per cent of gross sales was taxed as capital gains. This is lower than the dividend tax rate of 20 per cent, if actual capital gains exceeded five per cent of acquiring costs. If tax filing were selected, a capital-gains-tax rate of 26 per cent was imposed on profits (gross sales minus acquiring costs and any taxes and expenses). Therefore, this option was used for selling securities for losses or profits to be offset with losses. In the case of securities-capital gains, before 1988 the light taxation on capital gains might have encouraged individuals to invest more in securities, especially equities, as opposed to bank deposits. However, the tax rule changes in 1988 making capital gains more heavily taxed did not have any measurable impacts on stock investing behaviour or stock prices. When the expectation of stock price increase is so strong, moderate taxation may not readily dampen the expectation of profits, even though heavy taxation will destroy the market.

5. DID THE 'BUBBLE' CAUSE THE 'LOST DECADE'?

The bubble bursting is commonly blamed for the stagnant Japanese economy in the 1990s. However, several questions can be raised about this common explanation. Were asset price increases from 1985 to 1989 all bubble? Should a burst bubble necessarily result in economic stagnation for ten years? Could policies in the 1990s have revived the economy?

My assessment is slightly different from the conventional wisdom. The burst bubble problem was over by 1995, causing failures of several smaller financial institutions. The sorry state of the Japanese economy since 1995 is a result of weak fiscal, monetary, and supervision policies. This assessment is based on the observations that stock-price declines and their impact on corporations and banks were completed by 1995, and the problems of non-performing loans were clearly understood by 1995. If non-performing loans problems had been addressed in 1995–96, the picture would have been different. In a sense, the bursting of *the bubble* produced a malignant tumour, and there was a failure to remove it surgically before it spread further.

By 1992, stock prices were down by 60 per cent compared to the peak. Land prices were declining, but not as much as 60 per cent. (However, the land price index may have lagged behind the true transaction prices in the market, because transactions became rare in the process of the burst bubble, and the index was calculated from assessments by experts.) The range of the problems from over-investment in the real estate sectors to the non-performing loans problem among banks and non-bank banks became obvious by 1992. The fiasco of the public money injection in the *jusen* (housing loan companies) resolution process in 1995 set back serious efforts to clean up the banking system. (See Cargill et al., 1997, Ch. 6.) The burst bubble problem would have been much easier to deal with if funds were injected in 1995 in exchange for writing off non-performing loans to nip the problem in the bud.

Mistakes were made on the monetary-policy front throughout the decade. The monetary tightening in 1990–91 was slow to be reversed for fear of reviving a mini-bubble. Monetary policy remained cautiously tight in 1995–97. Fiscal policy was also tightened in April 1997. These factors contributed to the stagnant economic performance of the 1990s. The role of the burst bubble was almost over by 1995. The handling of a financial crisis in 1987–98 did not minimise losses for tax payers.

6. CONCLUDING REMARKS

After reviewing the Japanese experience of *the bubble* years, my conclusions are as follows:

(1) In order to limit damage to the economy from a bubble and burst bubble, it is important to build a resilient financial system, through strict supervision policy, so that asset price fluctuations will not weaken financial institutions. Supervision policy would include regulatory measures that would limit lending concentration and exposure to real-estate-related sectors.

(2) Monetary policy should pay attention to asset price movements. However, it may be difficult and inappropriate to raise interest rates sharply when the CPI inflation rate is low (below one per cent as in Japan), even though asset prices are increasing at 30–40 per cent.

(3) The official discount rate could have been raised in the summer of 1988 in Japan, when the Federal Reserve and Bundesbank raised interest rates. That would have slowed down the rise of stock and land prices, but *the bubble* was already large by then.

(4) *The bubble* is only partially responsible for *the lost decade*. A series of policy errors have made the small problem of a burst bubble much bigger than need have been the case.

REFERENCES

Cargill, T., M. Hutchison and T. Ito (1997), *The Political Economy of Japanese Monetary Policy* (Cambridge, Mass.: MIT Press).

Cargill, T., M. Hutchison and T. Ito (2000), *Financial Policy and Central Banking in Japan* (Cambridge, Mass.: MIT Press).

Cecchetti, S. G., H. Genberg, J. Lipsky and S. Wadhwani (2000), *Asset Prices and Central Bank Policy*, Geneva Reports on the World Economy, No. 2 (Geneva: International Centre for Monetary and Banking Studies).

Ito, T. (2001), 'How to Rescue Japan', Personal View (*Financial Times*, 23 October).

Ito, T. and T. Iwaisako (1996), 'Explaining Asset Bubbles in Japan,' *Monetary and Economic Studies* (Bank of Japan, Institute for Monetary and Economic Studies), **14** (July), 143–93.

Okina, K., M. Shirakawa and S. Shiratsuka (2001), 'The Asset Price Bubble and Monetary Policy: Japan's Experience in the Late 1980s and the Lessons,' *Monetary and Economic Studies* (Special Edition) (Bank of Japan, Institute for Monetary and Economic Studies), 19 (February), 395–450.

Ueda, K. (1990), 'Are Japanese Stock Prices Too High?' *Journal of the Japanese and International Economies*, **4**, 4, 351–70.

3

Why Does the Problem Persist?
'Rational Rigidity' and the Plight of
Japanese Banks

Kiyohiko G. Nishimura and Yuko Kawamoto

1. INTRODUCTION

JAPANESE banks have been in trouble for a long time.[1] In the crisis of
November 1997, Sanyo Securities, a mid-sized securities firm, Hokaido
Takushoku Bank, a city bank, and Yamaichi Securities, one of the then Big Four
securities houses, all collapsed within a three-week period. Following the crisis,
the government quickly arranged with the Bank of Japan and the Deposit
Insurance Corporation a transfer of 30 trillion yen: 17 trillion yen to protect the
depositors of failed financial institutions and 13 trillion yen to inject as capital
into under-capitalised banks. Of this public money, 1.8 trillion yen was then
injected into 18 major banks and three regional banks, all of which were rather
reluctant to receive it. This initiative did not resolve the problem, however, and
in 1998 the Government was forced to nationalise two failing banks, the Long-Term
Credit Bank and the Nippon Credit Bank, both of which had already received
public money. The Government increased the amount of public money available
from 30 to 60 trillion yen and encouraged banks to apply for a second subsidy.

KIYOHIKO G. NISHIMURA is from the University of Tokyo. YUKO KAWAMOTO is from
McKinsey & Company, Inc., Japan. They are grateful particularly to Benjamin Friedman and
Patrick McGuire and other Symposium participants for their valuable comments and suggestions,
to Takanobu Nakajima and Kozo Kiyota for permission to include part of an on-going joint
research project on individual firm dynamics, and Shin Kanaya for able research assistance. The
views expressed here are the personal views of the authors and in no way represent the views of
the institutions to which the authors belong.

[1] Hoshi and Kashyap (1999 and 2001, Ch. 8) provide vivid summaries of the development of the
troubled banking sector throughout the series of crises.

FIGURE 1
Squandering Past Legacies: Deteriorating Bank Profits, 1982–2001

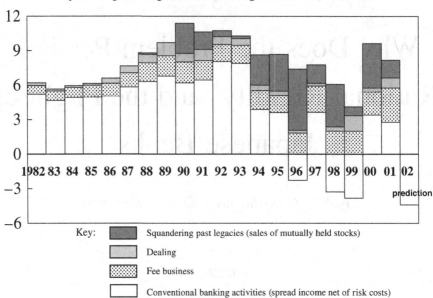

Key:

■ Squandering past legacies (sales of mutually held stocks)

▦ Dealing

▨ Fee business

☐ Conventional banking activities (spread income net of risk costs)

Sources: Calculations by the authors, based upon analysis of financial statements from all banks, various issues; *Nihon Keizai Shimbun*; disclosure papers of various banks; and McKinsey in-house analysis.

Fifteen major banks applied, again reluctantly, and received a total of 7.5 trillion yen. Yet again, this stopgap measure failed to resolve the problem. Non-performing loans that had persisted throughout the 1990s remained despite massive write-offs. New non-performing loans surfaced as old ones were written off. As of the time of writing (May 2002), it is widely recognised that the Japanese financial market problem is not over.

A remarkable feature of Japanese banking problems is the *persistence* of the apparently non-optimal and non-rational behaviour of Japanese banks. Figure 1 shows the authors' estimate of Japanese banks' gross profit rate and composition between 1985 and 2001. There is a remarkable contrast between the stable pattern of profits from conventional banking activities, dealing, and the fee business in the 1980s, and the deterioration of profitability of these 'core' banking activities after 1994.[2] Even more remarkable is the squandering of 'past legacies,' i.e., realised capital gains in the sales of stocks held mutually with their close trading

---

[2] There is consensus among economists that the government's slow, uneven and ad hoc approach to financial deregulation coupled with the banks' inability to adapt to changing market conditions brought about by this deregulation caused the sharp decline in the gross profit rate from conventional banking activities. See, for example, Hoshi and Kashyap (2001).

partners (some are *keiretsu* firms) that have consistently been used to prop up gross profits, particularly after 1994. For example, in 1996, 1998 and 1999 banks suffered losses in their conventional banking activities but managed to generate profit overall in this way. In 2002, even legal reserves were depleted for dividend payments. As President Nishikawa of Sumitomo Mitsui Bank laments: 'We have lost almost everything we had accumulated since the war. We are down to the bare bones' (*Nihon Keizai Shimbun*, 12 October, 2001).

Another example of apparently non-optimising and non-rational behaviour that is hard to understand in the logic of economics was witnessed at the very moment of the second banking crisis that occurred in 1998. In September of that year when taxpayers' money was being injected into the banks in order to re-capitalise them, President Masao Nishimura of the Industrial Bank of Japan made his famous comment about the Bank 'having a social responsibility to apply for tax money.' He said:

> This is not about the interests of one bank, but the interests of the entire Japanese economy and indeed the entire global economy. If we do not do this, we will be forced to accept re-capitalisation, so we must do it. The government has prepared 25 trillion yen and we have a social responsibility to receive that (quoted by Nihon Keizai Shinbun, 21 October, 1998)

This nebulous comment can only be understood when one accepts the idea that a bank is a 'public institution' not a private one.

In this paper we aim to give a 'rational' account for the apparently non-optimising and non-rational behaviour of Japanese banks, and to explain why their plight has been so prolonged and wide reaching despite ample and mounting evidence that they must change their business practices. In doing so, we depart from the mainstream of literature on Japanese banking, which is predominantly concerned with the close relationships between big banks and large corporations as exemplified by the debate over the main bank system and *keiretsu* financing.[3] Instead, we focus on the long-term relationships between banks and small to medium-sized enterprises, which account for almost half (49.45 per cent) of all loans made in the Japanese banking sector with paid capital of no more than 0.3 billion yen (in the case of wholesale trade, 0.1 billion yen); 5.6 per cent of loans are to enterprises with paid capital of 0.3 to 1 billion yen. Thus, for the banking sector as a whole, small to medium-sized enterprises are at least as important as large corporations. Moreover, large corporations such as Toyota and Sony started out as small enterprises. Thus, to capture the characteristics of Japanese banking as a whole it is important to understand the nature of banking with small to medium-sized enterprises in Japan.

---

[3] See Hoshi and Kashyap (2002) and references therein for theories and evidence stressing the importance of the main bank system and *keiretsu* financing. Also Miwa and Ramseyer (2001) for strong arguments against the same.

The paper is organised as follows. In Section 2, we develop a theory of community banking based on long-term relationships between banks and entrepreneurs, and explain the resulting rigidity even in the face of changing market conditions. We argue that this is a manifestation of rational rigidity in the Japanese economy and that it is particularly prevalent in the labour market. In Section 3, we explore the implications of this type of banking, and present three examples showing how it characterises the Japanese banking system. In particular, we explain that rational rigidity is likely to be institutionalised. We also explain how an expanding economy and ever-increasing asset prices made rational rigidity in the community banking viable until the collapse of the asset markets in 1990. In Section 4, we examine whether deteriorating financial positions in the 1990s had an adverse effect on banks' influence on individual enterprises, using large-scale panel data from Japanese enterprises. We show that, with the exception of a small number of large corporations in specific sectors, Japanese banks do rather well in their assumed role. The main problem, therefore, is not that Japanese banks are paralysed due to deteriorating financial conditions, but that their community banking business model with institutionalised rigidity is no longer profitable enough to sustain them. In Section 5, we look at changes that must be made to this model and discuss whether it should even be abolished altogether.

2. A THEORY OF COMMUNITY BANKING AND RATIONAL RIGIDITY

One of the most distinctive characteristics of the Japanese economy in the 1990s was its apparent long-term rigidity across many economic activities. For example, even after the so-called *bubble economy* burst at the beginning of that decade, many large firms have been reluctant until recently to change their wage and employment practices despite very weak market conditions. This persistence has puzzled economists because rational economic agents must adapt their practices to changing economic conditions all the time. This rigidity is apparent not only in the labour market but also in corporate management and the public sector.

We believe that the apparent inability of the Japanese banking sector to adjust to changing market conditions has its roots in the same rigidity seen in other industries. Employing and re-interpreting the rational rigidity model of Nishimura and Tamai (2001), we explain that the apparent long-term rigidity is in fact rational as long as large permanent changes do not occur. The argument is based on the logic of a long-term relationship between the bank and the debtors.

The model developed here may be considered as a 'community banking' model, in which we are concerned mostly with small to medium-sized firms or entrepreneurs as opposed to large corporations that have been the major focus of past studies. This segment is a useful focus for this study, which attempts to examine the effect of the Japanese banking system on all firms, not just large corporations, and to compare different effects of Japanese banking between small to medium-sized enterprises and large corporations especially in the 1990s. The model incorporates several institutional factors found in Japan.[4]

Let us first explain the rational rigidity theory in the framework of labour markets since rigidity is most pronounced in labour relations. The oft-cited merit of the long-term employer-employee relationship is that it enables workers to learn by doing in the production process, or in other words, it takes advantage of the so-called experience curve of workers. As a worker works longer with one firm, more firm-specific skills are acquired in the workplace. These skills increase the worker's productivity in the production process. In addition, these skills may reduce the worker's disutility of labour through better cooperation with co-workers. It has been argued that the advantage of long-term relationships is greater in Japan than in other countries for social and cultural reasons, thus explaining the prevalence and strength of the Japanese long-term employer-employee relationship. There is also ample evidence that learning-by-doing, or on-the-job training, is important in the Japanese workplace.

In this learning-by-doing process, the degree of skill acquisition is dependent on worker motivation and the resulting attentiveness. A motivated worker works more attentively, acquires more skills, and becomes more productive than a worker lacking in motivation. The dependence of learning-by-doing on worker motivation and worker attentiveness introduces an inter-temporal link: workers' high work attentiveness in the present implies acquisition of skills, which in turn increases productivity in the future. The firm can motivate the worker by offering an implicit long-term wage contract that pledges a higher wage in the future, rewarding high future labour productivity acquired through attentive work in the present. In fact, the practices of large Japanese firms can be viewed as long-term wage contracts in an implicit form. These firms have an age-related wage profile that is stable over set periods, allowing a worker to predict his future wage according to the length of time employed with the company.

This inter-temporal nature of learning-by-doing causes long-term rigidity. Because of the dependence of present work attentiveness on future productivity, the firm pledges high future wages to encourage learning-by-doing in the present. However, by the time a worker has accumulated skills, he has also grown older. The firm could cut his wages below the pledged level, but the worker cannot retaliate by lowering his skill accumulation, since he had already accumulated present skills and that there would be lower future skill acquisition anyway. A firm could theoretically increase profit by reneging on the implied contract.

---

[4] The details of the model, which is a reinterpretation of the long-term labour-market rigidity model of Nishimura and Tamai (2001), are available from the authors on request.

It is unlikely, however, that such opportunistic behaviour would pay off. It would jeopardise a firm's credibility and no worker would credit future wage pledges. In addition, learning-by-doing would be substantially reduced, adversely affecting the firm's long-term profits. If the long-term losses caused by the opportunistic behaviour outweigh its short-term gains as outlined in the previous paragraph, the firm would elect not to do it.

Suppose, then, that market conditions change unexpectedly. The firm, a rational economic agent, wants to adjust its wage policy for all employees, both younger and older, according to the new economic conditions. However, since a change in wages for older employees would constitute reneging on the long-term wage contract (the wage rate pledged in the previous period), the firm finds itself in a dilemma: does it adjust wages and trigger an adverse effect on future productivity, or stick to the current contract that is now inefficient? The firm has to make a rational choice between the two. Most Japanese firms opt for the latter, i.e., long-term rigidity, since the adverse effect on productivity triggered by any wage adjustment would be considerable in Japan.

This argument can easily be applied to a bank and its long-term relationship with small to medium-sized debtor-entrepreneurs, which might be called the community-banking model. Consider a bank and a set of entrepreneurs 'attached' to it, where the bank plays the same role as the firm, and the entrepreneurs are in the same position as the workers. The bank has a monopoly over supplying funds to these entrepreneurs. The bank is a going concern with infinite horizons, while new entrepreneurs are born and old entrepreneurs retire. The entrepreneur's performance in the market depends on his level of effort, just as the worker's productivity is determined by his attentiveness. Moreover, there is a similar inter-temporal link: the entrepreneur's management skills improve and his costs are reduced when he combines his efforts with the bank's advice and other services. Greater efforts today mean lower costs tomorrow and higher profits today. These joint proceeds are shared between the bank and the entrepreneur in various and subtle ways. For example, the bank may charge the entrepreneur various fees. In some cases, the entrepreneur may be asked to put his money in non-interest-bearing accounts.[5] In other cases, the entrepreneur may be encouraged to employ retiring bank employees or contribute to bank subsidiaries' activities. In addition, the entrepreneur undertakes efforts to expand his business so he borrows more from the bank, thereby contributing to the bank's profits. This borrowing cycle is probably the bank's biggest motivation to maintain a

---

[5] This arrangement is common. In the literature, it is considered a means to raise effective interest rates, but it is not clear why such a complicated scheme is employed instead of raising lending rates.

long-term relationship with the entrepreneur (although this is not explicitly considered in the Appendix model because of considerations of mathematical tractability).

So just as the firm encourages the worker's efforts by offering the promise of higher wages, so the bank can encourage the entrepreneur's efforts to incorporate the bank's advice in order to improve the firm's efficiency and expand its business, by rewarding these efforts through the promise of lower borrowing costs. In this way, the bank has a stake in the proceeds of the entrepreneur's improved management skills.

The bank then faces the same problems as the firm in the labour market. The bank encourages the entrepreneur's efforts by offering him an implicit 'long-term contract' which pledges lower borrowing costs in the future, rewarding high future efficiency acquired through his present efforts based on the bank's advice. However, once the entrepreneur has learned management skills and grown older, the bank could increase his borrowing costs with no fear of an adverse effect on management skill acquisition, and could thus increase its profits by reneging on the long-term implicit contract made with the old entrepreneur in the present. However, this cynical ploy would jeopardise the bank's reputation and no subsequent entrepreneur would believe the bank's pledge. Ultimately, such a move would result in lower management skill acquisition among its clients and ultimately lower profits for the bank. Thus, the bank, when it weighs long-term losses against short-term gains, is not likely to renege. Moreover, even when market conditions change unexpectedly, the bank is likely to honour its pledge, since any change to the old entrepreneur's interest payment scheme would constitute reneging on the long-term contract. The bank is therefore likely to employ rational rigidity as long as the change is not a large, structural one.

This 'community-banking' model can be considered as one variant of general relationship banking. However, the model differs from conventional relationship models in several ways (see the Appendix for further details). Firstly, entrepreneurs' profits are a joint-product of entrepreneurs' efforts and the bank's advice and other services. Secondly, entrepreneurs and the bank share this joint-product not only through interest payments but also various fees and other means. Thus, the bank-borrower relationship is not simply a loan contract. Third, the bank *always* has a short-term incentive to renege on the implicit contract and entrepreneurs know it. In a stable environment, the bank will not renege because it does not want to suffer the bad reputation that will result. However, in a rapidly changing environment, the bank may resort to reneging, and entrepreneurs may become sceptical about what a bank will do under such conditions. Then, both parties may agree to some institutional arrangements to prevent the bank's opportunistic behaviour in order to realise the joint-benefits of the bank-entrepreneur relationship.

3. RATIONAL RIGIDITY IN JAPANESE BANKING

a. Three Implications of the Community-banking Model

The theory of the community-banking model as just explained has three implications. First, the bank is likely to offer *a lower base-lending rate than would be offered by arm's-length banking,* to encourage entrepreneurs to acquire management skills. The bank gets its share of these improved skills not directly from a higher lending rate, but indirectly through, for example, fees and higher interest payments incurred by a greater borrowing volume.

Second, the bank tries to honour past pledges even if they are no longer optimal under changed market conditions. In arm's-length transactions, the bank is likely to call in firms' loans if they fail to repay their debts. Although we do not examine such cases explicitly in our formal model, rational rigidity results suggest that a bank maintaining long-term relationships with many entrepreneurs is not likely to take such an immediate disciplinary strategy, but instead will keep a distressed firm alive for a while to give it time to recover and to offer managerial advice; in this way the firm may recover from a temporary downturn and begin to repay its debts. And even if it eventually fails, the bank will have honoured its long-term pledge not to let the firm down, so it does not antagonise its current and potential trading partners. Consequently, *the rate of bankruptcy is substantially lower than in arm's-length banking.*

Third, the entrepreneur knows that the bank always has an incentive to renege on the implicit long-term contract, which makes the entrepreneur sceptical of any changes to that contract on the part of the bank. However, in some cases renegotiation of long-term contracts is mutually beneficial both for bank and entrepreneur when market conditions change. If there are institutional disincentives that stand in the way of the bank seeking to opportunistically maximise short-term profits, the entrepreneur is likely to believe the bank and mutually beneficial renegotiations can take place. Consequently, the bank is willing to honour these arrangements even though such institutional measures may pose additional constraints on their profit maximisation. Thus, the third implication of rational rigidity is that *institutional measures preventing short-term-profit maximisation are likely to emerge,* even though these measures constrain profit maximisation. In this way, 'rational rigidity' is institutionalised.

In this section, we explore evidence of these three implications of the community banking model within Japanese banking.

(i) Low base lending rate to small to medium-sized firms

There is strong evidence that the lending rate of Japanese banks is lower than the lending rate in arm's-length banking, in which the kind of long-term relationships observed in community banking does not exist. In Table 1, we take Standard

TABLE 1
Lending Rates for Segments of Borrowers

Rating	S&P Default Rate	Estimated Credit-Cost Rate	Actual Lending Rate	Default Probability Estimated from Historical Data
AAA	0.01	0.01	0.2	0.0
AA	0.03	0.03	0.3	0.0
A	0.06	0.06	0.4	0.0
BBB	0.26	0.22	0.625	0.01
BB	1.75	1.29	1.0	0.315
below B	5.04	3.50	1.5	2.08

Notes:
'S&P Default Rate' is 1-year rate calculated from S&P's global 3-year cumulative rate of default. 'Estimated Credit-Cost Rate' is the default rate minus the asset-collection rate (average collateral rate times collection rate) [authors' calculation]. 'Actual Lending Rate' is interview-based figures of big city banks.

Source: Standard & Poor's, *Rating Performance 2000 – Corporate Defaults: Will Things Get Worse Before They Get Better?*, 2001. Interviews conducted by the authors in September 2001.

and Poor's global rate of default for each category of borrowers, which is often taken as a benchmark for the default rate in other countries, in which arm's-length banking is the rule.[6] We then calculate the credit-cost rate, which is the default rate minus the asset-collection rate. It is evident that, for profit-seeking firms, the lending rate should exceed the estimated credit-cost rate substantially. In fact, the estimated credit-cost rate is higher if the borrower has a lower rating. Since many small to medium-sized enterprises have lower ratings in general, one would expect in arm's-length banking that the lending rate offered to them is substantially higher than that offered to large corporations with good credit rating.

In the third column of Table 1, we show the actual lending rate of Japanese banks. As this column shows, Japanese banks overall offer a lower lending rate than that offered in arm's-length banking. In fact, the actual lending rate is *lower* than the estimated credit-cost rate for categories BB and below B, which is striking. Moreover, the difference between the lending rate to large and high-rated corporations and to small and low-rated enterprises is remarkably small in today's Japan. These facts cannot be rationally explained without accounting for the role of long-term relationships as a critical factor in a Japanese bank's rate decisions.

One may wonder whether such low rates of community banking may jeopard-ise banks' profits. We estimate the default probability for each category from historical default rates, which is shown in the last column for the time period of

---

[6] The most appropriate way is to use Japanese default rates of arm's-length banking as a bench-mark. Unfortunately, we do not have such data in Japan, since arm's-length banking seems rather rare there. We use S&P rates, partly because of this data unavailability and partly because it has often been used recently as a practical benchmark for arm's-length banking in industry analyses.

around 2000. This shows that except for the 'below B' category, actual rates are higher than default probabilities. Thus, although the actual lending rates are low compared with 'global standard' rates incorporating the S&P rates, they are not grossly inconsistent with viable banking at least in the past. However, it is evident that profit margins are very slim, and moreover this backward-looking assumption of low default probability is rather misleading for the last few years, since bad loans have accumulated and a surge of bankruptcy is expected in the near future.

The incentive-inducing low-lending-rate strategy pays as long as the basic premise of the long-term relationship works, that is, as long as entrepreneurs eventually increase their management skills and expand their business to pay higher fees to and borrow more from the banks. In a rather continuously expanding economy with product-price inflation and asset-price inflation, this strategy works very well to increase the banking business. As shown above, this was the case until the collapse of the Bubble Economy in 1990 exerted prolonged, severe downward pressure on the economy.

(ii) Low rate of bankruptcy

Let us now turn to the second implication of the community-banking model – the lower rate of bankruptcy than in arm's-length banking. Table 2 shows the number of bankruptcies reported in Japan and the United States after 1987. It reveals a striking contrast between the two countries. In the period ending around 1989 – the heyday of the Japanese economy – the number of Japanese bankruptcies that led to liquidation or reorganisation is one fiftieth of the US total. Even in the depth of the prolonged stagnation in 1998, 3,508 Japanese enterprises went bankrupt, leading to liquidation or reorganisation, while in the height of the longest expansion, 37,113 US firms went bankrupt. Although there is a downward bias in the Japanese bankruptcy data,[7] it alone does not fill the huge gap between the two countries. Moreover, even if one takes account of simple disposition by suspension by bank credit, far fewer enterprises went bankrupt in the prolonged period of stagnation in Japan than in the longest boom in the United States.

One could argue against such international comparisons because they ignore vast differences in business practices across national borders (and a change in the US bankruptcy process in 1978). With this objection in mind, Table 3 compares the post-World War II era with the pre-World War II era. As is now well known (see, for example, Hoshi and Kashyap, 2001, Ch. 2 and references therein), the

---

[7] Japanese data are based on the surveys of Tokyo Shoko Research, commissioned by the Small and Medium Enterprise Corporation. All bankruptcies involving 10 million yen or more in debts are included nationwide. Those with smaller amounts are included only if the bankrupt enterprises are located in major cities. Thus, there is a slight downward bias since small-scale bankruptcies in small cities may not be properly covered by this survey.

TABLE 2
Bankruptcies in Japan and the United States, 1987–2000

Japan	Total	Quasi Chapter 7	Quasi Chapter 11	Others	Disposition by Suspension of Bank Credit	Grand Total
1987	1,310	668	214	428	13,736	15,046
1988	989	523	108	358	11,149	12,138
1989	649	356	63	230	8,010	8,659
1990	766	452	78	236	8,406	9,172
1991	1,156	768	159	229	12,422	13,578
1992	1,588	1,057	231	300	14,467	16,055
1993	1,836	1,124	274	438	13,976	15,812
1994	1,753	1,187	182	384	13,551	15,304
1995	1,944	1,369	185	390	14,149	16,093
1996	2,159	1,574	196	389	13,643	15,802
1997	2,978	2,164	278	536	15,268	18,246
1998	3,508	2,624	326	558	14,327	17,835
1999	3,457	2,516	218	723	13,668	17,125
2000	5,196	3,453	764	979	13,970	19,166

United States	Total	Chapter 7	Chapter 11	Chapter 12 + Chapter 13	Grand Total
1987	67,830	49,420	18,410	18,021	85,851
1988	55,816	39,808	16,008	10,292	66,108
1989	50,941	37,205	13,736	9,488	60,429
1990	54,453	36,667	17,786	10,068	64,521
1991	59,099	38,705	20,394	11,045	70,144
1992	58,537	38,467	20,070	13,144	71,681
1993	52,875	35,807	17,068	11,955	64,830
1994	44,160	30,781	13,379	10,232	54,392
1995	39,968	28,800	11,168	11,039	51,007
1996	41,647	30,289	11,358	11,826	53,473
1997	41,954	31,862	10,092	12,263	54,217
1998	37,113	29,229	7,884	9,977	47,090
1999	31,737	23,499	8,238	6,858	38,595

Notes:
'Quasi Chapter 7' includes Hasan ([legal] bankruptcy) and Tokubetsu Seisan (liquidation). 'Quasi Chapter 11' includes Kaisha Kosei (reorganisation and rehabilitation) and Wagi (composition).

Sources: Japan, Chusho Kigyō Jigyōdan (Japan Small and Medium Enterprise Corporation), and Kigyō Tōsan Chōsa Nenpō (Annual Report of Bankruptcy Companies), various issues. United States, data are supplied by Administrative Office of the United States Courts.

pre-World War II era was an era of active stock markets and passive banks. In particular, long-term stable relationships between banks and entrepreneurs, the hallmark of post-World War II banking, were not predominant if indeed they ever existed. Thus, if the post-World War II era has a substantially lower rate of bankruptcies than the pre-World War II era, then this suggests a genuine difference due to long-term relationships and their resulting rational rigidity.

TABLE 3

Creation and Destruction of Enterprises: Pre-World War II Era

Year	All Industries	By Industry					
		Agriculture	Fisheries	Mining	Manufacturing	Commerce	Transport
Rate of Net Increase							
1924–28	5.38	2.70	2.03	1.17	3.51	6.49	9.04
1934–40	0.40	−6.55	−0.43	16.62	3.09	−1.88	2.75
Rate of Creation (Rate of New Enterprises)							
1924–28	10.93	6.30	8.29	5.34	9.55	11.98	13.22
1936–40	9.25	5.09	7.79	19.93	11.32	7.76	9.88
Rate of Destruction (Estimated)							
1924–28	6.65	3.97	6.70	4.35	6.80	6.83	5.69
1936–40	8.97	9.43	8.10	5.77	9.09	9.07	7.81

Notes:

The rate of net increase is the change in the number of existing companies at the end of the fiscal year. The rate of creation is the ratio of newly-established companies to the existing companies. The rate of destruction is estimated from the rate of creation and the rate of net increase. The rates are the average of annual rates.

Source: *Shōkō Shō* (Ministry of Commerce and Industry), *Kaisha-Tōkei (Company Statistics)*, 1929 (22–25, 258–261), 1930 (22–25, 260–263) and 1945 (22–25, 364–365).

We take two periods in the pre-World War II era, 1924–28 and 1936–40. The first was after the Great Kanto Earthquake and just before the Great Depression, when stock markets were active. Stock prices rose by 19 per cent from 1924 to 1926 and were 10 per cent higher in 1928 than in 1924. The rate of destruction of enterprises in Table 3, estimated as the difference between the rate of new creation of enterprises and that of net increase, was 6.65 per cent, which is a substantial number. Thus, even in the era of booming stock exchanges, there were a sizeable number of bankruptcies in pre-war Japan.

In the 1936–40 period, which was just before World War II when war mobilisation efforts were getting started, the net increase of enterprises was almost zero. However, this was due to the balance between a high rate of creation and a high rate of destruction. The rate of destruction in the 1936–40 period was even higher than in the 1924–28 period, climbing to almost nine per cent annually.

In contrast, Table 4 shows that the post-war rate of destruction was far lower than that in the pre-war era. The rate of destruction is the ratio of the number of bankruptcies reported in Table 1 to the number of existing enterprises listed in the *Establishment and Enterprise Census*. The rate of destruction is 1.33 per cent in the relatively stagnant 1981–86 period, while the rate is 0.57 per cent in the Bubble Economy period between 1987 and 1991. These rates are substantially lower than in the pre-war era. The difference is all the more striking if one considers that non-performing loans surfaced and persisted in the 1990s. The rate of destruction is only marginally above its value in *the bubble economy*

TABLE 4

Creation and Destruction of Enterprises: Post-World War II Era

By Industry

Year	All Industries %	Construction %	Manufacturing %	Wholesale Trade %	Retail Trade %	Eating and Drinking Places %	Services %	Miscellaneous %
Rate of Net Increase								
1981–86	2.31	3.17	1.18	1.97	1.49	1.23	5.31	3.08
1987–91	3.25	5.26	2.09	1.66	1.30	4.53	6.04	4.72
1992–96	1.41	3.92	-0.30	-1.20	1.80	1.21	2.87	1.42
Rate of Creation (Estimated)								
1981–86	3.52	5.46	2.25	3.56	2.25	1.90	6.10	4.11
1987–91	3.76	5.98	2.53	2.48	1.62	4.80	6.39	5.28
1992–96	2.12	4.90	0.44	-0.08	2.16	1.55	3.40	2.19
Rate of Destruction (Bankruptcy Rate)								
1981–86	1.33	2.58	1.12	1.72	0.82	0.70	0.97	1.16
1987–91	0.57	0.88	0.48	0.88	0.33	0.33	0.44	0.68
1992–96	0.75	1.14	0.73	1.07	0.38	0.35	0.59	0.82

Notes:

The rate of net increase is change in the number of existing companies at each survey date. The survey of existing companies was undertaken as of 1 July in 1981, 1986 and 1991 and 1 October in 1996. The rate of destruction is calculated at the end of the fiscal year. Destruction means disposition by suspension of bank credit, [legal] bankruptcy, an application for composition, a ruling of reorganisation and rehabilitation or a ruling of liquidation. For destruction of enterprises with the total amount of the debt under ten million yen, 215 major cities are surveyed, while the whole country is surveyed for destruction with the debt no less than ten million yen. Thus, the rate of destruction is slightly under-estimated since destruction in small cities may not be properly counted. The rate of creation is estimated from the rate of destruction and the rate of net increase. The rates are the average of annual rates.

Source: For net increase and creation, *Sōmuchō* (Management and Coordination Agency), *Jigyōsho Kigyō Tōkei* (Establishment and Enterprise Census), 1981 (Vol. 3, Table 3), 1986 (Vol. 3, Part 1, Table 4), 1991 (Vol. 3, Table 3). For destruction, *Chusho Kigyō Jigyōdan* (Japan Small and Medium Enterprise Corporation), *Kigyō Tōsan Chōsa Nenpō* (Annual Report of Bankruptcy Companies), 1990 (Table 14-1) and 1997 (Table 14-1).

period, hovering at 0.75 per cent. The picture for individual industries is very similar.

What emerges from these tables is that banks in the post-World War II era have followed a strategy of keeping enterprises alive even when they are in financial difficulty. They give time and managerial advice so that the enterprises may recover from a temporary downturn and begin to repay their debts. Even if they cannot, banks avoid liquidating them and prefer to secure their money from the owner-managers and their relatives, who are sureties-liable jointly and independently for the enterprises' debts. Their collateral against such debts is usually real estate and listed-firms' stocks. As long as stock prices and, in particular, property prices increase, this strategy works very well. Thus, this system of *soft* disciplinary action by banks[8] worked well when asset prices followed a sharp upward trend until the collapse of the asset markets in 1990.[9]

(iii) Institutionalisation of rational rigidity

In the community-banking model of Section 2, the entrepreneur knows that if his relationship is taken in isolation, the bank has an incentive to renege on the implied long-term contract, and he is sceptical of the bank's proposal to make any changes in the implicit contract. In other words, the long-term contract that the bank offers to one generation of entrepreneurs is time-inconsistent. It becomes time-consistent only in the context of overlapping generations of entrepreneurs who would view the bank badly if it reneged, leading to a substantial decline in long-term profits.

In some cases, renegotiation of long-term contracts is beneficial mutually for bank and entrepreneur when market conditions change. However, often only the banks are aware of the changes, and they are faced with the problem of credibly conveying that a change has occurred while avoiding the misperception that it wants to exploit the ignorance of the entrepreneur. If there are institutional measures that serve as disincentives against the bank's short-term profit maximisation, the entrepreneur is likely to believe the bank and mutually beneficial renegotiations take place. Consequently, the bank is willing to honour these arrangements even though such institutional measures may pose additional constraints on their profit maximisation. Thus, the third implication of the community-banking model is institutionalisation of rational rigidity: that is, institutional measures prohibiting short-term profit maximisation are likely to emerge, even though these measures may constrain overall profit maximisation.

---

[8] 'Soft' for enterprises, but not for their owner-managers who are often obliged to pay their enterprises' debts personally. The practice of making owner-managers liable for their enterprises' debts also helps to curtail the opportunistic behaviour induced by limited liability.

[9] However, it should be kept in mind that the evidence of low bankruptcy is consistent with any theory of relational banking explaining banks' reluctance to write off bad loans, and thus does not distinguish the community banking theory as opposed to other relational banking theories.

In fact, a distinctive characteristic of Japanese banking is the strong emphasis on its role in the community. The idea that 'profits are important' cannot be taken for granted in the Japanese finance industry, as can be seen from statements made by top bank managers. Former President Hiroshi Kurosawa of the Industrial Bank of Japan, for example, said:

> Profit is very important. Our profit is too small. But profit is not the 100% purpose of IBJ – it is not a purely commercial bank. Our philosophy is to serve our clients and Japanese industry. There must be profit, but profit must be reasonable. If we make too much profit, we are eating our clients' profits. We do not like to maximise our profits. (*Euromoney*, February 1998).

These ideas and sensibilities have been cultivated and shared by the industry for decades.

The basic conceptual framework for Japanese bank management places 'profit' and 'public-interest' in opposition, with the public nature of financial institutions often serving as an antidote to 'excessive' emphasis on profit. This emphasis on 'public interest' is institutionalised and clearly cited in the *Banking Law*.

Article 1, Paragraph 1 of this law states:

> In light of the public nature of the banking business, the purpose of this law is to provide for sound and appropriate management of banking services and to contribute thereby to the sound development of the national economy by maintaining trust and protecting depositors so as to facilitate finance.

The emphasis is clearly on banking safety and the public interest. *Paragraph 2* attempts to harmonise the public nature of banking with the private nature of banking companies:

> The administration of this law shall take care to respect self-directed efforts in the management of the banking business.

The combined need to assure public interest and safety in banking while maintaining the nature of banks as private companies is behind the extraordinarily ambiguous and cryptic phrase 'take care to respect.'

The textbooks that new bank employees use to study for the certificate examination on 'basic banking operations' also touch on the public nature of banks, but do so only in the most nebulous and vague terms. One textbook[10] says:

> These three principles, public interest, safety and profitability, have aspects that contradict each other. Therefore, banks must be managed in ways that harmonise the three principles. The specific ways in which this is done will change according to changing economic and financial circumstances.

In another section, it comments:

> In other words, past practice was to give primary emphasis to assuring the public nature and safety of banking by placing restrictions on the scope of business in which banks could engage, with respect to the types of financial products and services they could offer, and the ways in which they set their prices.

---

[10] *Kinyū Ginkō Kentei Senta* (Centre for Testing Banking Skills), editor, *Kinyū Keizai no Kihon* (*The Basics of Banking*, 1990, p. 170).

It goes on to cite recent changes such that:

> In recent years, however, there has been a growing tendency to respect the self-directed efforts of banks. The stiff regulations of the past have been loosened and new freedom and flexibility have been brought to banking supervision and the banking industry. When the banking business was subject to a plethora of regulations, business results were judged in terms of amounts of deposits and loans. Recently, however, more weight in the evaluation of business results is being placed on earnings, profit margins and other elements that have to do with profitability.

However, this passage is also vague and does not clarify whether banks as private enterprises should maximise profits or, equally, shareholder value.

This strong emphasis on 'public interest' versus profit in Japanese banking is in stark contrast to banking in other countries. In the United States, banks are regulated to ensure that they provide safe and sound banking, monetary and financial stability, an efficient and competitive financial system, and protection of consumers from abuse by financial institutions, as exemplified in the Banking Act of 1933:

> An act to provide for the safer and more effective use of the assets of banks, to regulate interbank control, to prevent the undue diversion of funds into speculative operations, and for other purposes.

However, no clause places 'public interest' above profit in importance. The same is true in France and Germany, with the possible exception of the regional savings banks law *Sparkassengestz*. These banks are obliged to serve public interest and be non-profit organisations. However, they are not private but public banks, and Brussels has now decided to abolish them.

4. WERE JAPANESE BANKS PARALYSED IN THE 1990s?

The collapse of stock and real estate markets around 1990 and the subsequent stagnation of the economy posed a serious problem for the community-banking business model of Japanese banks. As discussed in the previous section, a growing economy (that encourages more borrowing by entrepreneurs) and rising asset prices (that make write-offs of bad loans possible without imposing outright bankruptcy on failing enterprises) are two pillars that support the community-banking business model and the resulting rational rigidity. These two pillars collapsed simultaneously on a dramatic scale.

The magnitude of the stock market's collapse is well documented, but that of property prices may be grossly under-estimated. As of March 2002, the Nikkei index stands at less than one-third of the peak it hit in 1990. According to the published land price officially reported by the Land Agency (now the Ministry of Land, Infrastructure and Transport), the average land price also shows a similar drop. However, these official published price data tend to under-estimate the

FIGURE 2

Market Land Price and Published Land Price: Central Tokyo Commercial Area
1975–99 (1975 = 1)

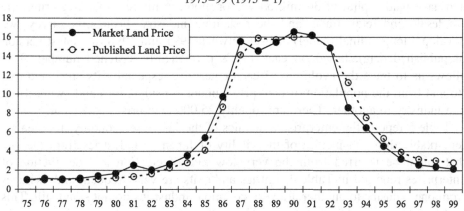

changes in transaction prices. The average land price based on this data source (and similarly appraisal-based price data sources) conceals the severity of the downturn in commercial areas where collateral properties (so important in Japanese banking as explained) are usually located. Figure 2 compares the hedonic price index based on actual transaction prices and the index based on published prices in the central Tokyo commercial area. The magnitude of the decline is even more striking and the under-estimation of the change in the official price data is apparent. The transaction-price index is now *one-eighth* of its peak value of 1990, though the published price index is one-fifth of its peak value. These officially published prices are misleading and are one reason why the severity of non-performing loans was overlooked in the early stages of the banking crisis.[11] The dramatic collapse of the asset markets coupled with a very weak real economy in the 1990s is responsible for rapidly deteriorating bank profit as exemplified in Figure 1 in the Introduction.

A logical question arises: did this profit pressure disrupt the Japanese banking's long-term relationship? In other words, did the non-performing loan problem paralyse Japanese banks and cause a serious problem in industrial adjustment in the 1990s? We look at this question in the remainder of this section.

It should be noted that we are not concerned with large corporations but with all enterprises: simply looking at firms listed on major stock exchanges[12] is not enough. To do this, we use the *Kigyō Katsudō Kihon Chōsa (The Basic Survey*

---

[11] This is clearly stated in the Study Project on the Effect of Balance Sheet Adjustments (2001).

[12] Several studies to do this have emerged in recent years. For example, see Kobayashi et al. (2002).

of Japanese Business Structure and Activities)[13] micro-database. This is, in fact, a truncated census that covers *all* enterprises that employ 50 workers or more and have paid capital of 30 million yen or more, in mining, manufacturing, the wholesale and retail trade, and the restaurant industry. From this survey, we develop a longitudinal (panel) dataset between 1991 and 1998 (the latest version of published data), based on each firm's permanently assigned number. This allows us to trace the evolution of each enterprise, especially its entry and exit (to and from the population of enterprises under consideration) and switch from one industry to another. There are roughly 25,000 enterprises each year.

Table 5 reports the enterprise dynamics of the Japanese economy. It reveals a remarkably different picture of the vitality of Japanese industries from the one that might be inferred from the very low rate of creation and destruction of enterprises reported in Table 4. Entries and exits are very frequent and switches from one industry to another are very common; industries do not stand still. This is the picture of real industry dynamics in Japan: enterprises are very active in entry, exit and switching. Therefore the picture painted of extremely stable Japanese industries in Table 4 is deceptive: it only accounts for births and deaths, but, once born, enterprises engage actively in industrial dynamics.

The active movement of enterprises requires finance. This suggests that Japanese banks may play an important role in making these very active industrial dynamics possible. In fact, for small to medium-sized enterprises, entry and switching would be difficult without bank financing.

To examine this connection, we constructed a panel of enterprises having sufficient financial data from the previous panel of enterprises, and examine whether the rate of return on tangible assets (ROA) is influenced by the way investment is financed (equity-financed, debt-financed (= bank financed), or internally financed).[14]

The results are shown in Table 6. Because of limited space, we only report industries showing statistically significant differences in the effect of various financings. There are two major findings.

---

[13] This survey is conducted by the Research and Statistics Department, Minister's Secretariat, Ministry of Economy, Trade and Industry (METI). It was first conducted in 1991, again in 1994, and has been conducted annually since then. Financial information (simple versions of balance sheets) is available for each firm as well as revenue, employment and cost data. The strength of the survey is its (even if truncated) census coverage and the reliability of its figures. We drop firms that have missing values in employment, tangible assets and capital statements.

[14] The base case is internal financing. We consider an equity-financing dummy (EFD) and a debt-financing (bank-financing) dummy (DFD) in the case of positive gross investment, and a debt-financing working-capital dummy (WDFD) in the case of zero investment, and try to discern the effect in conjunction with an industry switch dummy (Switch) and restructuring dummy (Restruct). We also consider the effect of large corporations by the cross-term with a Large Firm dummy. They are all one-period lagged dummies. We also include labour-to-capital ratio, the root of the size of tangible assets, age of enterprise, foreign equity share, debt-capital ratio, and year dummies to control macroeconomic factors. It is a fixed-effects model estimated by instrumental variable methods taking account of possible simultaneity problems.

TABLE 5

Entry and Exit Patterns of Japanese Enterprises 1991–98: Non-financial Firms Employing 50 or More Total and Major SNA Industries

	Ratio of Entry to End-of-Period Total (Annual Rate)			Ratio of Exit to Beginning-of-Period (Annual Rate)		
	Entry Total	From Other	From Outside	Exit Total	From the Industry	To Outside
1991–94 Industry						
All industries	6.1%	–	6.1%	5.2%	–	5.2%
Food products and beverages	7.8	2.0	6.0	7.6	2.0	5.8
Textiles	6.5	1.9	4.8	8.7	2.6	6.6
Chemicals	6.0	2.4	3.8	5.4	2.3	3.2
Fabricated metal products	10.3	5.2	5.6	10.5	6.5	4.6
General machinery	8.8	4.2	4.9	8.6	4.3	4.5
Electrical machinery	8.3	3.9	4.7	8.0	3.1	5.1
Transportation machinery	8.0	3.6	4.6	6.9	2.7	4.2
Construction	19.7	4.6	16.3	12.4	4.0	5.2
Wholesale trade	8.5	2.6	6.1	8.2	2.7	5.7
Retail trade	8.4	2.8	5.9	7.8	2.8	5.2
1995–98 Industry						
All industries	5.9%	–	5.9%	6.1%	–	6.1%
Food products and beverages	7.4	1.6	6.0	7.1	1.8	5.5
Textiles	6.4	1.6	4.9	9.9	2.0	8.4
Chemicals	5.0	2.0	3.1	6.0	2.1	4.1
Fabricated metal products	8.6	4.0	5.0	8.8	3.5	5.7
General machinery	8.4	3.6	5.2	8.4	3.3	5.4
Electrical machinery	7.6	2.3	5.5	8.0	3.2	5.1
Transportation machinery	6.9	2.7	4.4	6.9	2.7	4.4
Construction	8.4	4.9	3.9	10.3	3.5	7.5
Wholesale trade	8.0	2.6	5.7	8.7	2.3	6.7
Retail trade	8.7	2.3	6.6	8.4	2.5	6.2

Notes:

All non-financial enterprises employing no less than 50 employees are counted. 'Entry' of an enterprise is new appearance of the particular firm. 'Exit' of an enterprise is its disapperance. Industry classifications here are based on 23 SNA industry classifications.

Source: Authors' calculation from individual enterprise data in *Kigyō Katsudō Kihon Chōsa (Basic Survey of Japanese Business Structure and Activities)*, 1991, 1994–98.

First, banks seem to have a positive impact on enterprises that are changing their product mix (and thus switching from one industry to another) and those that are 'restructuring' themselves in certain industries. Here 'restructuring' means a decrease in the value of the tangible assets that the enterprises possess and includes activities such as sales of plants and buildings.

The table shows that the cross-term of the debt-financed-investment dummy and the industry-switch dummy is positive and statistically significant in the

TABLE 6
Results of Instrumental Variable Fixed-effect Regression: Selected Industries
(Only Finance-related Dummy Variables are Shown)

	Pulp, Paper and Paper Products	Chemicals	Petroleum and Coal Products	Fabricated Metal Products	Precision Machinery	Construction	Wholesale Trade	Real Estate	Transport and Communications
EFD × Switch	-1.572	-1.535	-0.476	0.731	1.491	6.389	6.447	-1.411	-1.833
	[0.06]	[0.53]	[0.08]	[0.08]	[0.37]	[0.19]	[0.51]	[0.57]	[0.60]
DFD × Switch	-0.595	7.274***	-0.213	-5.174*	-2.200*	-11.133	-0.791	1.053	2.321
	[0.05]	[7.24]	[0.11]	[1.71]	[1.94]	[0.95]	[0.23]	[0.68]	[1.31]
WDFD × Switch	-0.633	0.727	12.487***	1.493	-0.928	88.454***	-2.82	-0.181	
	[0.02]	[0.28]	[3.08]	[0.22]	[0.37]	[2.85]	[0.45]	[0.49]	
EFD × Restruct.	0.681	0.025	-0.011	0.246	-1.653	-2.403	-0.285		1.589
	[0.06]	[0.02]	[0.00]	[0.05]	[1.20]	[0.15]	[0.08]		[0.56]
DFD × Restruct.	5.589*	0.473	-0.062	0.201	0.164	-0.754	1.973*	0.183	2.381***
	[1.87]	[1.47]	[0.09]	[0.15]	[0.39]	[0.14]	[1.74]	[0.91]	[2.95]
WDFD × Restruct.	2.215	0.204	2.443	-2.431	-0.327	-34.396***	3.767**		0.133
	[0.27]	[0.16]	[1.35]	[0.82]	[0.33]	[3.29]	[2.31]		[0.03]
EFD × Switch × LargeFirm		1.736	0.894	0.81	-2.292	16.094	-31.442		
		[0.34]	[0.09]	[0.03]	[0.33]	[0.22]	[1.60]		
DFD × Switch × LargeFirm		-7.145***	-0.119	5.299	8.792	17.974	64.343***		-2.778
		[2.62]	[0.02]	[0.40]	[1.07]	[0.35]	[5.99]		[0.60]
WDFD × Switch × LargeFirm							4.963		
							[0.11]		
EFD × Restruct. × LargeFirm	1.756	0.006	0.167	0.411	1.502	-19.907	2.411		-1.426
	[0.10]	[0.00]	[0.04]	[0.06]	[0.54]	[0.45]	[0.35]		[0.29]

DFD × Restruct.	-5.003	-0.286	-0.372	-0.016	-0.529	-4.722	4.875	-1.399***	-2.105
	[0.58]	[0.49]	[0.19]	[0.00]	[0.44]	[0.25]	[1.33]	[3.73]	[1.10]
× LargeFirm		1.293		4.376					
		[0.27]		[0.13]					
WDFD × Restruct.						26.618			
						[0.35]			
× LargeFirm							-6.495		
							[0.49]		
Observations [number of firms times time periods]	1,649	3,608	2,634	3,709	1,300	1,722	24,785	92	296
Number of firms	540	1,114	901	1,336	466	654	8,694	46	113
R-squared	0.23	0.57	0.11	0.39	0.26	0.38	0.1	0.99	0.01

Notes:
1 Absolute values of t-statistics are in brackets. *, **, *** indicate significant at 10, 5 and 1 per cent, respectively.
2 EFD = Equity-Financed Investment dummy, DFD = Debt-Financed Investment dummy, WDFD = Debt-Financed Working-Capital dummy (when (gross) investment is equal to zero). They take value of 1 if they are observed one year before, 0 if otherwise.
3 Switch dummy is 1 if the enterprise switched from one industry to another one year before, and 0 if otherwise. Restructuring dummy is 1 if the value of tangible assets decreases, and 0 if otherwise.
4 LargeFirm dummy takes the value of 1 if the enterprise has more than 10 billion yen in paid capital and 0 if otherwise.
5 Other explanatory variables included in the regression analysis but not shown here are L/K, root of K, Enterprise Age, Foreign Equity Share, Debt-Capital Ratio, Year Dummies of 1996, 1997 and 1998, and Constant, where L is the number of workers and K is the value of tangible assets.
6 Industries having statistically significant coefficients in some of the dummy variables are shown.
7 Method: Fixed-Effect Instrument Variable Estimation with $L/K(t-1)$ and $K^{1/2}(t-1)$ used as instruments.

Source: Individual enterprise data in *Kigyō Katsudō Kihon Chōsa* (Basic Survey of Japanese Business Structure and Activities) between 1994 and 1998.

chemical industry, while the cross-term of the debt-financed investment and the restructuring dummy is positive and statistically significant in pulp, paper and paper products, wholesale trade, and transportation and communications. This finding is remarkable since one quarter of all non-financial firms under consideration (fifty workers or more with paid capital of 30 million yen or more) are wholesale trade enterprises. Moreover, the cross-term of the debt-financed-working-capital dummy and industry-switch dummy is positive and statistically significant in petroleum and coal, and construction. These results suggest that the positive effects of long-term relationships persisted even into the difficult 1990s.

However, there are also downsides. The cross-term of the debt-financed-working-capital dummy and the industry-switch dummy is negative and statistically significant in fabricated metal and precision. The cross-term of the debt-financed-working-capital dummy and the restructuring dummy is negative and statistically significant in construction. This result shows that the banking sector has uneven results in encouraging its debtors to make sensible decisions.

Second, there is evidence that the benefit of long-term relationships is not felt in large corporations, and there is a strong indication that banks are simply pumping money into failing large firms. The cross-term of the debt-financed-investment dummy and the industry switch dummy is negative in chemicals, while the cross-term of the debt-financed-investment dummy and the restructuring dummy is negative and statistically significant in real estate. These results are consistent with the conventional wisdom that banks are extending loans to keep failing large corporations afloat in the real estate industry. However, it should also be noted that banks seem to play a positive role for large wholesale trade corporations.

It is not true, therefore, that Japanese banking was paralysed in the 1990s and failed in all industries to materialise the benefits of long-term relationships. In some industries banks have had a productive influence on their debtors.

5. CONCLUSION

One of the most perplexing factors in Japanese financial crises is the *persistence* of the apparently non-optimal and non-rational behaviour of Japanese banks. We have provided a rational explanation for this behaviour based on a theory of community banking: the long-term relationships between banks and small to medium-sized entrepreneurs that result in rational rigidity in lending. We have identified three clear implications of community banking – a low lending rate, a low bankruptcy rate, and in particular, institutionalisation of rational rigidity (pledge of no profit maximisation) – as these prevail in the Japanese banking system. We have also argued that the community-banking-business model was sustainable so long as the economy rather continuously expanded and asset prices went up, which was the case before the asset markets crashed in 1990. Thus, the stagnation and free-falling asset prices of the 1990s imposed serious strains on the Japanese banking system. However, we have also found that banks continued their community banking role into the 1990s at least partially, although there are also indications that they failed to restructure failing enterprises in industries such as construction and real estate. So, the problem was not that paralysed banks were blocking recovery (although this might be true in some of the industries mentioned above), but that the current community-banking-business model is no longer sustainable as private enterprises in the market economy now suffer from asset price deflation and economic stagnation.

To gauge the magnitude of the problem, we calculate possible losses that the present practices inflict on bank profits as follows: we assign enterprises to appropriate credit-rate classifications and estimate the distribution of loan balances over these classifications. Then we apply the rates on the distribution reported in Table 1 and calculate possible gains and losses (the amount of spread income (or loss) between the actual lending rate and the credit-cost rate), *assuming that Standard and Poor's global default rate is the true rate in Japan*. The result is staggering. The possible losses due to insufficient spread (or, to be precise, negative spread) over the credit cost rate amount to some 3.5 trillion yen!

This figure is tentative, and admittedly grossly overstated, since we assume that Standard and Poor's global rate is *the* Japanese rate. This clearly ignores the difference in business practices between Japan and other countries and it is grossly different from the historical rate. However, the magnitude of losses is unlikely to disappear even if we adjust the numbers to current Japanese circumstances, if one properly considers mounting bad loans and a resulting surge of bankruptcy rates predicted in the near future. We are in a stagnant economic situation that prevents profitable lending and are facing asset-price deflation that makes recovery of non-performing loans through the sale of property collateral difficult.

This suggests that institutional change may be necessary to make Japanese banks profitable again. Such a change is likely to include a major modification to community-banking practices, if not their outright abolition. At the very least, the range of these practices may be substantially reduced and banks engaging in such activities may be transformed into quasi-non-profit community organisations. In the majority of lending, banks may raise lending rates to low-rated firms to reflect an increase in the bankruptcy rate in these categories. Moreover, some of the existing loans may be securitised with fair market values and sold to institutional investors. Through these fundamental steps, banks may be relieved from long-term risks or uncertainty, that has overshadowed Japanese banks for more than a decade. It will be a formidable challenge to take these steps and at the same time to keep conventional long-term relationships, so that some banks may move from the old practices all the way to a market-oriented, arm's-length banking. Thus, a monolithic structure of Japanese banks, in which all banks seem to engage in community banking, may be replaced by heterogeneous banking activities. Simply bailing out the banks as they are with injections of public money will not resolve the problem unless there is a major shake-up in current banking practices.

REFERENCES

Hoshi, T. and A. Kashyap (1999), 'The Japanese Banking Crisis: Where Did It Come From and How Will It End?' in B. S. Bernanke and J. Rotemberg (eds.), *NBER Macroeconomic Annual*, **14**, 129–201.

Hoshi, T. and A. Kashyap (2001), *Corporate Financing and Governance in Japan* (Cambridge: MIT Press).

Kobayashi, K., T. Saito and T. Sekine (2002), 'Forbearance Lending: A Case for Japanese Firms,' Working Paper 02-2E (Bank of Japan).

Miwa, Y. and J. M. Ramseyer (2002), 'The Fable of the Keiretsu,' *The Journal of Economics and Management Strategy*, **11**, 169–202.

Nishimura, K. G. and C. Shimizu (2002), 'Distorted Land-Price Information,' in K. G. Nishimura (ed.), *Economic Analysis of Japanese Real Estate Markets* (Tokyo: *Nihon Keizai Shimbun*, June, in Japanese).

Nishimura, K. G. and Y. Tamai (2001), 'Long-Run Rigidity in Labour Markets,' in T. Negishi, R. Ramachadran and K. Mino (eds.), *Economic Theory, Dynamics and Markets* (Boston: Kluwer Academic Publishers).

Study Project on the Potential Influence of Balance Sheet Adjustment (Chair: K. G. Nishimura) (2001), *The Effects of the Disposition of Non-Performing Loans*, report submitted to Economy and Finance Minister Heizo Takenaka (June).

4

Japan's Fiscal Policies in the 1990s

Toshihiro Ihori, Toru Nakazato and Masumi Kawade

1. INTRODUCTION

JAPAN'S fiscal situation in the 1990s was the worst of any G7 country, having deteriorated rapidly with the collapse of the 'bubble economy' in 1991 and the deep and prolonged period of macroeconomic recession which ensued, and from which recovery has been slow and modest despite the implementation of counter-cyclical Keynesian policy. In order to evaluate the recent movement of fiscal policies in Japan, it is useful to consider the following points. How did the counter-cyclical Keynesian policy such as raising public expenditures and reducing taxes matter in the 1990s? Has fiscal sustainability become a serious issue? Is it really necessary to reduce fiscal deficits? How much was the optimal deficit in the 1990s? Did the fiscal reconstruction movement in 1997 cause the recession? Why did it fail? This paper will address these issues.

Let us first summarise briefly the recent movement of fiscal deficits and fiscal reform in the 1990s. After the 'bubble economy' was broken in 1991, the resulting tax decreases reduced revenue. At the same time the politico-economic pressures for larger expenditure budgets and counter-cyclical packages of fiscal measures intensified. Responding to them, the Ministry of Finance (MOF) employed several measures for stimulating aggregate demand. However, as will be shown in Section 2, these counter-cyclical Keynesian measures were not especially effective and resulted in an increase in the fiscal deficit.

The planned bond-dependency rate rose from a low-point of 7.6 per cent in fiscal year (FY) 1991 (initial) to 18.7 per cent in FY 1994 (initial). The reality was still worse. The implementation of counter-cyclical fiscal policy through supplementary-budgets in-year led to further borrowing still, and the actual bond-dependency rate was more than 22 per cent in FY 1994.

TOSHIHIRO IHORI and MASUMI KAWADE are from the University of Tokyo. TORU NAKAZATO is from Sophia University, Tokyo. They thank Tamim Bayoumi, James Hines and other Symposium participants for useful comments.

The state of the national finances deteriorated rapidly throughout FY 1995 and FY 1996. The MOF was forced to borrow 22.0 trillion yen to finance a deficit swollen by the large fiscal stimulus in September 1995, resulting in a bond-dependency ratio of 28.2 per cent, its highest level since 1980. In FY 1996 the planned issue of 10.1 trillion yen of special deficit bonds exceeded all previous experience. Despite the gravity of the fiscal situation, the initial budgets for FY 1996 and 1997 nevertheless provided for further increases of expenditure, of 5.8 per cent and 3.0 per cent, respectively. Not only were fixed costs for prior commitments rising, those for discretionary expenditures continued to rise as well. The servicing of that debt absorbed more than a fifth of the total general account budget.

The FY 1998 initial budget was drawn up making utmost efforts to deal with the macroeconomic and financial situation within the framework of new fiscal austerity. The Fiscal Structural Reform Act, which was implemented in November 1997, had three targets to be achieved by FY 2003: (1) elimination of special balanced bonds; (2) reduction of the general government debt-GDP ratio to 60 per cent; and (3) reduction of general government deficit-GDP ratio to three per cent.

General expenditures were down 1.3 per cent over the FY 1997 initial budget, the largest decline in history. However, as will be explained in Section 5, in the light of the severe economic and financial situation, the Fiscal Structural Reform Act was revised in May 1998, so that income tax reductions could be easily implemented. Furthermore, since the Liberal Democratic Party (LDP) lost the upper house election in July 1998, the new Prime Minister Obuchi changed the target of fiscal policy. Namely, further tax reductions and increases in public works were implemented to stimulate aggregate demand, following the traditional Keynesian counter-cyclical policy. In FY 1998 the issue of special deficit bonds was 21.7 trillion yen due to several fiscal policy measures. By the end of FY 1999 the accumulated debt total was 327 trillion yen, equal to 65 per cent of GDP. The deficit on the general government financial balance in FY 1999 was 10.0 per cent of GDP, with a gross debt of over 108 per cent. The Fiscal Structural Reform Act is not regarded as a legal constraint any more.

2. EVALUATION OF THE KEYNESIAN EFFECT

a. Method of Analysis

Based on the above discussion, we will analyse empirically the macroeconomic effects of fiscal policy. There exist competing arguments on the efficacy of fiscal policy in the 1990s. One hypothesis is that the effects of fiscal policy were very large and hence recession would have deepened without fiscal expansion. Alternatively, it may be that fiscal policy did not have enough of an expansionary effect to push up macroeconomic activity, and hence unlimited public expenditures simply made the fiscal crisis worse. These opposing arguments, which have different policy implications, are mostly due to different understanding of the appropriate macroeconomic analytical framework. Namely, the former hypothesis is based on the conventional Keynesian model of liquidity-constrained agents, while the latter is based on the neoclassical model of rational agents.

Although there have been many controversial arguments on the effectiveness of fiscal policy in the 1990s, statistical evaluation has not been well implemented. Due to the limited availability of time-series data concerning Japan's fiscal policy in the 1990s, it is difficult to estimate quantitatively how effective Keynesian fiscal policy was during the period. In order to evaluate empirically the effect of counter-cyclical fiscal policy, it is useful to decompose the relevant macro-economic and fiscal data into trend and cyclical components. Since the trend component reflects a long-term change, we can treat it as the structural change. We then consider how Japan's fiscal policy actually stabilised cyclical components of the macroeconomic variables in the context of a VAR analysis.

There are several popular filtering methods to decompose time-series data into trend and cyclical components, including the Hodrick-Prescott filter (HPF) and the Band-Pass filter (BPF). First, we decompose the time-series data using these filters. Then, we examine the impact of the fiscal variables of the cyclical component on macroeconomic activities by using vector-auto regression (VAR) and impulse response functions. Since our aim is to clarify the impact of fiscal policies without prior information, we adopt non-structural VAR estimation.[1] The variables used are: private consumption (CP), private investment (IP), public investment (IG), tax revenue (GR), and export (EX) and import (IM). To decide the order of the lags, we use the Akaike Information Criterion (AIC) and Schwarz's Bayesian Information Criterion (SBIC) criteria.

b. Results

The estimated impulse responses are shown in Figures 1–4. Since the results in the BPF case are almost the same as those in the HPF case, we do not show the BPF case explicitly in these figures. The results in the 1990s are different from those in the pre-1990 period.[2] A one per cent increase in public investment decomposed by the HPF (or BPF) case would marginally stimulate private consumption in the 1990s but depress private consumption before the 1990s[3] (see

---

[1] Using the VAR method, Ihori and Kondo (2001) analyse the effect of public investment on private consumption. Kato (2001) and Ramaswamy and Rendu (2000) also analyse the macro-economic effect of fiscal policy in a similar way.

[2] The results in the 1990s are almost stable when we change the starting period to any year between 1985 and 1995. Because our main purpose is to investigate the effects in the 1990s, we have chosen the above estimation-period decomposition.

[3] Ihori and Kondo (2001) estimate the effect of public capital on consumption by incorporating public capital into the utility function and point out that it has been falling since 1965. Kato (2001) estimates the effects of government consumption and public investment based on the structural VAR and points out that they fell considerably after 1985.

FIGURE 1
Impulse Response of 1 Per Cent Impact of Public Investment on Private Consumption

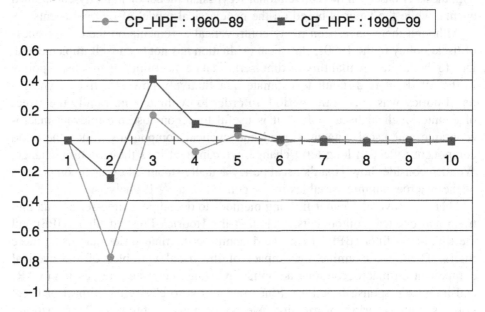

FIGURE 2
Impulse Response of 1 Per Cent Impact of Public Investment on Private Investment

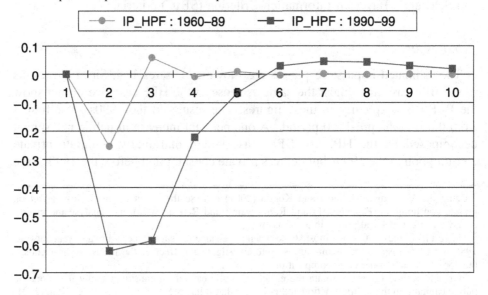

FIGURE 3
Impulse Response of 1 Per Cent Impact of Revenue on Private Consumption

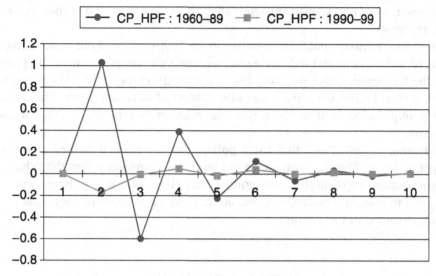

FIGURE 4
Impulse Response of 1 Per Cent Impact of Revenue on Private Investment

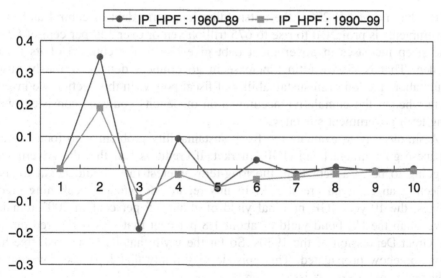

Figure 1). Figure 2 suggests that the crowding-out effect on private investment became larger in the 1990s.

We then estimate the impulse responses of the tax increase. The impact of tax revenue in the 1990s was smaller than before. As shown in Figure 3, a one per cent increase in tax revenue raised private consumption for the following quarter before the 1990s, while it had little effect in the 1990s. The effect on private investment was not significant. Actually, the effect was sometimes positive (see Figure 4).[4]

In short, increasing public investment in the 1990s crowded out private investment to some extent and did not increase private consumption much. It appears that the Keynesian effect was not observed strongly in the 1990s. Moreover, the adverse (non-Keynesian) effect was often observed in recent years. The overall policy implication is that the Keynesian fiscal policy in the 1990s was not effective.

Bayoumi (1999) shows that fiscal policies have generated limited effects on output in Japan. That is, tax policies did not have a stronger effect than changes in government expenditure. Furthermore, the effect of fiscal policies was too marginal to stimulate macroeconomic activity, which is consistent with the main results obtained in this section.

3. FISCAL SUSTAINABILITY

a. Method of Analysis

By the end of FY 2001, the outstanding long-term debt of central and local governments is projected to rise to 675 trillion yen or over 130 per cent of GDP. The steep increases in government debt give rise to the concern of its future burden. That is, the resulting increase in government deficits seriously raises doubt about the long-run sustainability of fiscal policy. In this section we investigate whether the cumulative accumulation of deficits could be consistent with long-term government solvency.

A simple way to evaluate the fiscal sustainability problem is to focus on the Japanese government bond (JGB) market. If creditors fear that the government is going to be in a debt trap, the long-term interest rate should begin to rise, reflecting an enlarged credit risk. In this regard, despite its weakening credit ratings, the 10-year JGB nominal yield of about 1.5 per cent in 2002 remains lower than the US bond yield of about 1.8 per cent that was registered during the Great Depression of the 1930s. So far the myth that JGBs are risk-free has been somehow propagated. This episode may imply that Japanese government solvency is not a serious issue at present.

---

[4] Ramaswamy and Rendu (2000) point that the slowdown of private investment was the main reason in the recession in the 1990s, and fiscal expansion did not have much effect in spite of its scale.

TABLE 1
The Test for Government Solvency: Estimated Coefficient of β

	(1) 1957–93	(2) 1957–94	(3) 1957–95	(4) 1957–96	(5) 1957–97	(6) 1957–98	(7) 1957–99
$r - n$ 0.01	0.0142 (0.726)	0.0305 (0.435)	0.0291 (0.395)	0.0294 (0.387)	0.0376 (0.272)	0.0524 (0.172)	0.0610 (0.142)
$r - n$ 0.02	0.0083 (0.641)	0.0160 (0.336)	0.0149 (0.292)	0.0151 (0.276)	0.0197 (0.167)	0.0271 (0.096)	0.0304 (0.087)
$r - n$ 0.03	0.0058 (0.565)	0.0104 (0.256)	0.0094 (0.213)	0.0096 (0.193)	0.0125 (0.102)	0.0017 (0.053)	0.0187 (0.053)
$r - n$ 0.04	0.0043 (0.498)	0.0072 (0.194)	0.0063 (0.158)	0.0064 (0.136)	0.0083 (0.063)	0.0112 (0.030)	0.0120 (0.032)
$r - n$ 0.05	0.0032 (0.441)	0.0051 (0.146)	0.0043 (0.120)	0.0043 (0.099)	0.0055 (0.040)	0.0074 (0.018)	0.0078 (0.020)
$r - n$ 0.06	0.0023 (0.391)	0.0036 (0.109)	0.0030 (0.096)	0.0029 (0.075)	0.0036 (0.026)	0.0048 (0.011)	0.0051 (0.013)

Notes:
The data of central and local governments are used in the estimation. All data are annual series. In parentheses below each coefficient is the p-value for the null hypothesis. $r - n$ = nominal interest rate – nominal growth rate.

However, we also have to consider the possibility that the performance of the JGB yield may not accurately reflect its credit risk. The Japanese banking sector continues to purchase JGBs simply because short-term capital gains from JGBs have been an easy option to offset existing losses from their holdings of equities. The low level of bond yields may in themselves represent 'bubbles.'

In this section we will attempt an alternative approach to test the fiscal sustainability condition, using the methods developed by Hamilton and Flavin (1986).[5] We conduct the empirical analysis outlined in the Appendix for the Japanese fiscal data from 1957 to 1999. To conduct the test, the values for the nominal growth rate, n, and the nominal interest rate, r, must be specified. Our strategy here is to set various values for $r - n$ and to check whether the results are sensitive to the values chosen.

b. Results

The results for each sample period are given in Table 1. The estimated results in columns (1)–(4) imply that the null hypothesis cannot be rejected at a five per cent significance level, suggesting that government solvency was not a serious problem until FY 1996. On the contrary, the result for the period 1957–1997 (column (5)) rejects the null hypothesis when $r - n$ is above 0.05, and the results

---

[5] For a recent analysis of Japan's government solvency, see also Ihori and Sato (2002).

for the period 1957–1998 and the period 1957–1999 (columns (6) and (7)) also reject the null hypothesis when $r - n$ is above 0.04. These observations indicate that fiscal sustainability may become a serious issue. The longer the sample period, the more likely we face a fiscal crisis. It follows that further fiscal expansion may cause a public debt crisis to occur in the near future.

4. OPTIMAL BUDGET DEFICITS

a. Method of Analysis

Even if the accumulation of public debt may still be sustainable, the expansionary fiscal policy in the 1990s has another problem. Prolonged excessive budget deficits are harmful for the economy in the sense that excessive deficits today mean higher marginal tax rates tomorrow, which may then result in higher deadweight-welfare losses of taxation in the long run.

To assess whether budget deficits are excessive, we can employ the theory of tax smoothing originated by Barro (1979). The idea is as follows. Since tax collections are distorting, a benevolent government should choose tax rates to minimise the present discounted value of the welfare loss. If the excess burden of taxation is a convex function of the tax rate, an optimal fiscal rule is to smooth tax rates over time and to finance the resulting differences between government expenditures and tax revenues by debt issuance. Using this analytical framework, we compare the actual deficit with the optimal one.

b. Results

Figure 5 plots the optimal and actual deficits as a fraction of GDP in terms of the optimal primary budget surplus, s^*, and the actual primary budget surplus, s. As explained in Section 1, the actual deficit has grown sharply due to a series of fiscal expansions since FY 1992. The optimal deficit has also gotten in step with the actual one, reflecting the prolonged economic downturn. Figure 5 suggests that the overall fiscal policy in Japan was implemented in consideration of the tax-smoothing hypothesis.

However, it should also be stressed that the actual deficit in the late 1990s was not desirable. The actual deficit has exceeded the optimal level during most of the late 1990s. For instance, the actual deficit was larger than the optimal one by one per cent of GDP in FY 1999. This implies that the Japanese government should have raised tax revenue of about five trillion yen from the viewpoint of the tax-smoothing consideration. As shown in Section 2, tax increases would have scarcely dampened macroeconomic activity. Such tax increases would have improved long-term economic welfare.

FIGURE 5
Actual and Optimal Budget Surpluses, 1955–2000

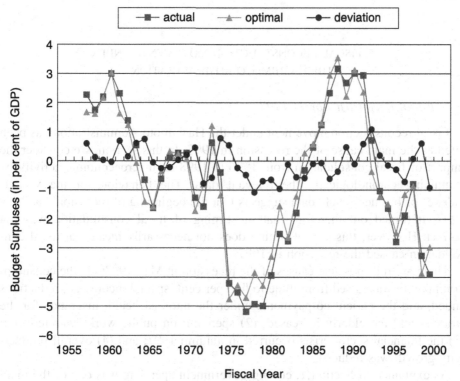

As shown in Section 3, the ballooning public debt may bring about a sustainability crisis. The tax-smoothing hypothesis is meaningful only if the sustainability condition is satisfied.[6] Moreover, in this section we focused on tax policy, leaving public spending policy intact. It is well recognised in Japan that government expenditure, especially spending on public works, becomes more wasteful as budget deficits become larger.[7] Thus, considering these factors, the optimal

---

[6] It is well known in the recent literature on optimal taxation, which relies heavily on the Ramsey-type growth model, that the government should impose high tax rates on all forms of capital early in its planning horizon, run a surplus, and then lower both tax rates asymptotically to zero and use the surplus to finance future government spending. When we incorporate this aspect, the optimal deficit in the 1990s may well be smaller than in Figure 5.

[7] There are many empirical studies on the productivity effect of public capital in Japan. See Iwamoto (1990), Asako et al. (1994), Mitsui and Ohta (1995), Yoshino and Nakano (1996), Doi (1998), Ihori and Kondo (2001) and Ihori and Sato (2002). They commonly conclude that public capital was productive, but that its productivity has greatly declined in recent years.

level of government deficit may well be much smaller than the result shown in Figure 5.

5. FISCAL RECONSTRUCTION MOVEMENTS UNDER
THE HASHIMOTO ADMINISTRATION

a. Fiscal Reconstruction in 1997

Fiscal reconstruction movement under the Hashimoto Administration has been cited as the main cause of the recession in 1997. In this section, we consider the impact of fiscal consolidation from 1996 to 1998 on macroeconomic activity by examining chronologically the relevant data. The behaviour of the various indexes of business cycle data suggests that the beginning of recession was May 1997. It turned out therefore that the timing of fiscal consolidation was not correct. However, this fact of timing does not necessarily mean that fiscal consolidation caused the recession in 1997.

There are four possible causes of the recession in May 1997: (1) the consumption tax rate was raised from three to five per cent, special income tax reductions ended, and the patient co-payments under the national health insurance for the workers and the elderly increased; (2) spending on public works was reduced; (3) the financial sector crisis occurred in autumn 1997; and (4) overall productivity growth was reduced.

As explained in Section 1, cutting government spending was one of the main targets of the fiscal-reconstruction movement started by the 'Fiscal Restructuring Targets' in 1996. The Fiscal-Structural-Reform Conference was organised in January 1997 and discussed the specific reduction targets for major expenditures. But, three weeks after the Fiscal Structural Reform Act was enacted, Prime Minister Hashimoto announced a special income tax cut. The total economic measure, which aimed at a Keynesian fiscal policy, was scheduled when the budget requests for fiscal 1997 were approved. Under these circumstances, the Fiscal Structural Reform Act was suspended in practice. So, it is inappropriate to say that the fiscal reconstruction movement had a negative effect on Japan's economy.

Based on the data decomposition in Section 2, we can observe the impacts of the consumption-tax increase and expiration of the special income-tax cut in April 1997 on macroeconomic activity. We found that the trend component of private consumption (growth rate of consumption) began to decline after the 1st quarter of 1996. It recovered slightly just before the 1st quarter of 1997 and declined rapidly in the 2nd quarter of 1997. Overall, it did not have a distinctive effect on consumption during this period. It suggests that the negative impacts of fiscal reconstruction were partial. The behaviour of the cyclical component shows this conjecture more clearly; private consumption sharply recovered in the

2nd quarter of 1997. Although private consumption was front-loaded and then reduced in early 1997, it returned to the usual trend. In addition, several indexes of production and employment did not get worse.[8] Watanabe et al. (1999) show that the impact of the permanent tax increase on consumption was very large.[9] Our result indicates that the impact of raising the consumption-tax rate from three to five per cent in 1997 was a temporary shock.

On the side of fiscal policy, we found that the growth rate of public investment began to decline after the 4th quarter of 1996. Additionally, the trend component of public investment declined by the early 1990s, but it stabilised after 1997. On the other hand, the cyclical component has fluctuated since 1995, reflecting instability in fiscal management. We also found that the growth rate of tax revenue began to decline from the 3rd quarter of 1995 and became negative in the 1st quarter of 1997. The cyclical component of tax revenue turned positive in the 2nd quarter of 1997. This indicates that the negative effects of fiscal reform lasted for a very short time. These findings suggest that discretionary fiscal expenditure did not have a strong effect on macroeconomic activity.

In November 1997, several large financial companies went bankrupt and trend consumption decelerated. Simultaneously, most indexes of production and employment worsened at that time,[10] and exports decreased. Under these circumstances, uncertain prospects of firms and the bad condition of exports caused private investment to decline. To summarise the results, based on examination of several important indexes of macroeconomic activity, the major cause of the recession in 1997 was not the fiscal reconstruction movement.[11]

b. Failure and Political Factor

Why did the fiscal reconstruction movement in 1997 fail? Certainly, the bad macroeconomic situation contributed to the failure. In addition to this, we would include the political factor.

When the government debt becomes large and the fiscal crisis becomes serious, it is more difficult to induce all interest groups to cooperate. In other words, the later the fiscal reconstruction movement begins, the more likely an unsuccessful

---

[8] In the 3rd quarter of 1997, the real growth rate was 6.9 per cent.

[9] Meredith (1998) also points out that the impact of the demand-stimulus policy from 1990 to 1996 by 5 per cent of GDP was to increase GDP by 3 per cent, while the fiscal consolidation policy from 1996 to 1997 by 2 per cent of GDP decreased GDP only by 1.25 per cent.

[10] Fear of a financial system crisis arose as follows: the Sanyo Securities went bankrupt on 3 November; the Hokkaido Takushoku Bank transferred its own business to the Hokuyo Bank on 17 November; and the Yamaichi Securities, which was the third major securities firm, announced bankruptcy on 24 November.

[11] Hayashi and Prescott (2002) suggest that economic stagnation in the 1990s was not attributed to a breakdown of the financial system but to a declining productivity-growth rate.

outcome. The free-riding problem in the fiscal reconstruction process is aggravated when players' choices are conditional on the observable collective variables. Ihori and Itaya (2001) compared the open-loop solution and the closed-loop solution for fiscal reconstruction. They found that, without commitment, higher existing privileges and higher government debt are made relative to the enforceable commitment case. When political leadership is weak under a coalition government, it is difficult to control the free-riding behaviour of interest groups. As shown in Doi et al. (2002) and Ihori et al. (2001), this factor cannot be ignored in Japan.

When the programme of fiscal reconstruction is too flexible in the sense that it allows each interest group to reconsider predetermined policies such as subsidy cuts at each point in time when the outcome of fiscal reconstruction is revealed, it is highly likely that fiscal reconstruction ends finally in failure. The Fiscal Structural Reform Act in 1997 had weakness in that it allowed for much room for reconsidering fiscal reform. Allowing such a possibility would strengthen the incentive of each group to free ride.

In order to realise a successful outcome, therefore, we have to remain with the long-term programme for fiscal reform that has been agreed at the beginning of the planning period. In practice, one effective means is to enact legislation for fiscal reform, which does not permit much room for reconsidering or revising the fiscal reconstruction plan. In terms of intergovernmental financing, the central government needs to restrain the lobbying activities of local political groups. Reforming the local allocation tax system so that each local government has to collect taxes to finance its own spending is also useful.

6. CONCLUDING REMARKS

It is true that the current macroeconomic situation in 2002 remains severe. But, it may also be true that Japan would face more difficult economic problems in the future since the population is ageing very rapidly and the Japanese market system is behind the 'global standard.' Even if it is needed to stimulate aggregate demand, the traditional Keynesian policy seems ineffective, as we have noted in Section 2. Furthermore, when the fiscal situation becomes very serious, fiscal reconstruction may stimulate private consumption and investment due to the 'non-Keynesian' effect. The results in Section 2 suggest that the 'non-Keynesian' effect has some relevance in the 1990s.

Public opinion concerning the role of government has changed significantly in Japan. The number favouring small government has become predominant in the business community. This change is probably caused by the fear that further increases in fiscal burdens would result in bankruptcy of the Japanese government, as suggested in Section 3. This concern provides background for the fiscal reconstruction and structural reform movement by the current Koizumi Administration.

There have been some attempts for such reform. For example, an effort is being made to put additional priority on infrastructure investment to improve people's lives and the environment in urban areas. At the same time, seeking to enhance both efficiency and transparency, the efforts to reduce costs and to utilise cost-benefit analysis have been complemented by a new re-assessment system. These changes are desirable but the speed of structural reform is not great. Further determined efforts are needed to reform public spending and taxation in a more efficient way. The most important policy lesson from fiscal policy in the 1990s is that long-run structural reform is more important than short-run Keynesian policy.

APPENDIX

Hamilton and Flavin (1986) develop the idea of verifying whether the intertemporal budget constraint of public sector would be satisfied. The budget constraint at time t can be written as:

$$T_t + B_{t+1} = G_t + (1 + r)B_t \tag{A1}$$

where B_t is the stock of government debt at the beginning of period t, G_t is government expenditure, T_t is tax revenue, and r is the fixed nominal interest rate. Dividing (A1) by GDP yields:

$$t_t + b_{t+1} = g_t + (1 + r - n)b_t \tag{A2}$$

where lowercase letters denote corresponding variables expressed as a fraction of GDP and n is the fixed nominal growth rate.

A general class of solutions to (A2) can be written as:

$$b_t = \sum_{i=1}^{\infty} (1 + r - n)^{-i} s_{t+i-1} + \beta(1 + r - n)^t \tag{A3}$$

where s_t is the primary surplus at time t ($s_t = t_t - g_t$). The sustainability condition is satisfied if the null hypothesis H_0: $\beta = 0$ is accepted.

When the assumption of perfect foresight is dropped, an expectation operator conditioned on the information set available at time t is generally added to (A3). If expectations of future budget surpluses are conditioned on past budget surpluses, s_{t-i}, and past government debts, b_{t-i}, then (A3) takes the following form:

$$b_t = \alpha + \beta(1 + r - n)^t + \gamma_1 b_{t-1} + \cdots + \gamma_p b_{t-p} + \delta_1 s_{t-1} + \cdots + \delta_p s_{t-p} + \varepsilon_t. \tag{A4}$$

Therefore, we can test the fiscal sustainability condition by estimating (A4) and checking whether the null hypothesis H_0: $\beta = 0$ can be rejected.

REFERENCES

Asako, K., A. Tsuneki, S. Fukuda, H. Teruyama, T. Tsukamoto and M. Sugiyama (1994), 'Productivity Effect of Public Capital and Welfare Evaluation of Public Investment Policy,' *Keizai Bunseki*, **135** (Economic Planning Agency, in Japanese).

Barro, R. (1979), 'On the Determination of Public Debt,' *Journal of Political Economy*, **87**, 940–71.

Bayoumi, T. (1999), 'The Morning After: Explaining the Slowdown in Japanese Growth in the 1990s,' National Bureau of Economic Research, Working Paper 7350.

Doi, T. (1998), 'Panel Analysis of Public Capital in Japan,' *Kokumin Keizai*, **161**, 27–52 (in Japanese).

Doi, T., T. Ihori and H. Kondo (2002), 'Government Deficits, Political Inefficiency, and Fiscal Reconstruction in Japan,' *Annuals of Economics and Finance*, **3**, 169–83.

Hamilton, J. and M. Flavin (1986), 'On the Limitations of Government Borrowing: A Framework for Empirical Testing,' *American Economic Review*, **76**, 808–16.

Hayashi, F. and E. C. Prescott (2002), 'The 1990s in Japan: A Lost Decade,' *Review of Economic Dynamics*, **5**, 206–35.

Harvey, A. C. and A. Jaeger (1993), 'Detrending, Stylized Facts and the Business Cycle,' *Journal of Applied Econometrics*, **8**, 231–47.

Ihori, T. and J. Itaya (2001), 'A Dynamic Model of Fiscal Reconstruction,' *European Journal of Political Economy*, **17**, 779–97.

Ihori, T. and H. Kondo (2001), 'Efficiency of Disaggregate Public Capital Provision in Japan,' *Public Finance and Management*, **1**, 161–82.

Ihori, T. and M. Sato (eds.) (2002), *Government Deficit and Fiscal Reform in Japan* (London: Kluwer).

Ihori, T., T. Doi and H. Kondo (2001), 'Japanese Fiscal Reform: Fiscal Reconstruction and Fiscal Policy,' *Japan and the World Economy*, **13**, 351–70.

Iwamoto, Y. (1990), 'On the Evaluation of Japanese Public Investment Policy,' *Economic Review*, **41**, 250–61 (in Japanese).

Kato, H. (2001), 'A Structural VAR Approach to Evaluate the Effects of Fiscal Expenditure,' National Institute of Population and Social Security Research Discussion Paper (in Japanese).

Meredith, G. (1998), 'Fiscal Policy: Summary of Staff Views,' in B. A. Bijan, T. Bayoumi and G. Meredith (eds.), *Structural Change in Japan: Macroeconomic Impact and Policy Changes* (Washington, DC: International Monetary Fund).

Mitsui, K. and K. Ohta (1995), *Productivity of Public Capital and Public Finance* (Nihon Hyoron Sha, Tokyo, in Japanese).

Ramaswamy, R. and C. Rendu (2000), 'Japan's Stagnant Nineties: A Vector Autoregression Retrospective,' *IMF Staff-Papers*, **47**, 259–77.

Yoshino, N. and H. Nakano (1996), 'Interregional Distribution and Productivity Effect of Public Investment,' *Financial Review*, **41**, 16–26 (in Japanese).

Watanabe, K., T. Watanabe and T. Watanabe (1999), 'Tax Policy and Consumer Spending: Evidence from Japanese Fiscal Experiments,' National Bureau of Economic Research, Working Paper 7252.

5

Japan's Negative Risk Premium in Interest Rates: The Liquidity Trap and the Fall in Bank Lending

Rishi Goyal and Ronald McKinnon

1. INTRODUCTION

SINCE the asset price bubble burst in the early 1990s, Japan's economy has been virtually stagnant and its banking sector has been troubled. Since the late 1990s, the macroeconomic performance has deteriorated and the banking sector troubles have worsened. The government has resorted to expansionary monetary policy and has tried expansionary fiscal policy. However, these standard stabilisation tools have failed to stimulate the economy. Most existing analyses have emphasised the need for broad-based structural reforms to clean up the banking sector and to liberalise various sectors of the economy. Others have emphasised the need for an even more expansionary monetary policy to halt deflation.

We believe that this emphasis on structural reform and further monetary (or fiscal) 'expansion' is misplaced.[1] In this paper, we argue that long- and short-term nominal interest rates in Japan have been compressed to historically low levels – the so-called liquidity trap – because of pressure coming through the foreign exchanges. This pressure has several facets. The first facet is the declining nominal interest rate on dollar assets from inflation stabilisation in the United

RISHI GOYAL is from the International Monetary Fund and RONALD McKINNON is from Stanford University. They are grateful to Andrew Coleman, Dale Henderson and other Symposium participants for helpful comments. The International Centre for the Study of East Asian Development, Kitakyushu, Japan, provided generous financial support.

[1] Structural reforms are needed to raise Japan's long-term trend growth rate and its real return on capital. However, our argument is that such reforms are not central to addressing the current problems of deflation and macroeconomic instability in the economy.

FIGURE 1
Growth of Bank Credit and Monetary Aggregates, 1980–2000

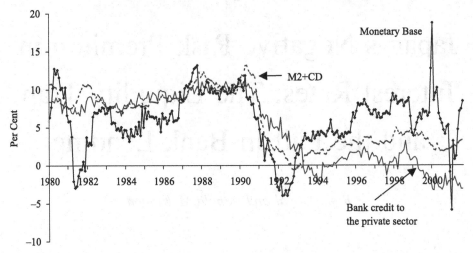

Note:
Twelve-month growth rates are computed.

Source: Bank of Japan.

States in the 1990s. The second is a *negative* risk premium in Japanese interest rates that has kept yields on yen assets well below those on dollar assets. The third facet is a residual fear, now possibly quite small, that the yen will resume appreciating secularly.[2] This paper focuses on the domestic financial consequences of the negative risk premium arising from the cumulative effect of more than 20 years of Japanese current-account surpluses.

As long-term interest rates have been pushed to very low values, short-term interest rates have been reduced to zero and Japan has found itself in a liquidity trap, where the Bank of Japan has been unable to halt deflation even though it has been increasing the monetary base at a high rate in the past few years – see Figure 1, and the more extensive depiction of Japan's very high growth in base money over the past decade in Shirakawa (2001).[3] In addition to the impotence of monetary policy at the zero lower bound of nominal interest rates, the compression of lending interest rates toward zero has squeezed bank-profit margins. This compression has made new bank lending hardly profitable, and has made

---

[2] This fear of an ever-higher yen was central in the earlier work of McKinnon and Ohno (1997 and 2001).

[3] Critics of the Bank of Japan (BoJ) argue that it is able to re-inflate the economy even at zero short rates. But their formal models, such as the ones discussed in Krugman (1998) and Svensson (2001), do not show how the BoJ would be able to re-inflate the economy (or depreciate the exchange rate) when short-term interest rates are trapped at zero.

it practically impossible for Japanese banks, by themselves, to gradually write off old bad loans out of current earnings. In many countries beset by bad loan problems, the spread between deposit rates and lending rates has been raised so that banks have been able to gradually recover loan losses with the passage of time. In Japan, however, the compressed spreads have hindered banks saddled with sizeable non-performing loans from earning profits that could be used to restore their capital. It also explains the slump in new bank credit to Japan's private sector.

The rest of the paper elaborates on and discusses these arguments. Section 2 presents the theory of the negative risk premium, along with supporting evidence and the theory's implications for the liquidity trap. It summarises a more detailed analysis provided in Goyal (2001). Section 3 discusses the consequences of compressed spreads for the banking system, and is the core contribution of this paper. Section 4 concludes with policy implications.

2. THEORY OF THE NEGATIVE RISK PREMIUM

Consider the plot of nominal interest rates on long-term US government bonds and long-term Japanese government bonds (JGBs) in Figure 2. Note two properties. First, since the late 1970s, Japanese rates have been well below US rates. Second, there has been a trend decline in the level of the interest rate in the United States and in Japan since the early 1980s.

FIGURE 2
Long-Term Interest Rates

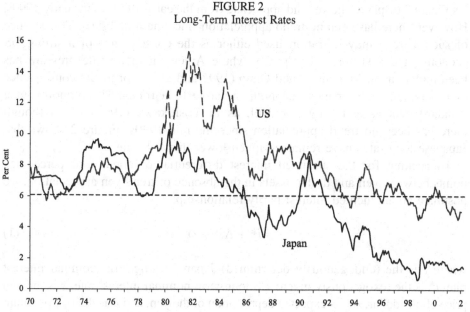

Source: International Financial Statistics, IMF.

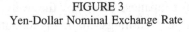

FIGURE 3
Yen-Dollar Nominal Exchange Rate

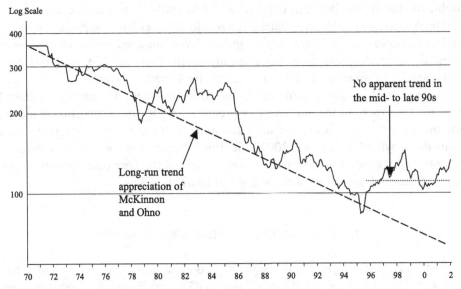

Source: International Financial Statistics, IMF.

Uncovered interest parity suggests that the interest differential should correspond to expected yen appreciation; otherwise, there would be arbitrage opportunities. As Figure 3 displays, the yen did appreciate from the early 1970s to the early 1990s. However, there has been no trend appreciation since the mid-1990s. The absence of such a trend may be rationalised either as the consequence of a strong US economy and a strong dollar policy where American mercantile pressure has been muted, as in McKinnon and Ohno (1997 and 2001), or as the consequence of a stagnant real Japanese economy relative to a robust US economy in a standard neoclassical growth model, as in Yoshikawa (1990). Even though there has been no trend appreciation since the mid-1990s, Figure 2 shows that Japanese long rates have remained much lower than US rates.

To account for the sustained interest differential of about four percentage points between yen and dollar assets in the absence of trend yen appreciation, we postulate an augmented interest parity relationship:

$$i = i^* + \Delta s^e + \varphi \tag{1}$$

where i is the (endogenously determined) Japanese long-term nominal interest rate, i^* is the (exogenously given) US long-term nominal interest rate, s is the yen price of one dollar, Δs^e is expected depreciation of the yen, and φ is the risk premium on yen assets. The interest differential, $i - i^*$, from the 1970s to the early 1990s was driven primarily by the negative Δs^e term. Since the mid-1990s, $\Delta s^e \approx 0$ and the interest differential has been driven primarily by the φ term, which is also negative.

φ is the excess yield that an investor demands for bearing foreign exchange risk. For a private Japanese financial institution holding net dollar assets, fluctuations in the yen-dollar exchange rate result in fluctuations in the yen value of the net dollar assets, and hence of the net worth of the financial institution. From its perspective, the dollar asset is the risky asset because its liabilities are denominated in yen. So, φ captures the excess yield, over and above expectations of ongoing yen appreciation, that the dollar asset must pay in order to induce the financial institution to hold it.

It follows that φ is negative for a creditor country such as Japan whose credits are denominated in foreign currency. Conversely, φ is positive for a debtor country whose debts are denominated in foreign currency. The size of φ depends on the share of net foreign currency assets or the net foreign currency debts and on the expected variance in the exchange rate. The larger the share of net foreign currency assets (debts), the more negative (positive) is φ. Hence, φ is inversely related to the net foreign currency asset position.[4]

These properties are in line with general, cross-sectional evidence provided by Lane and Milesi-Ferretti (2001) showing an inverse relationship between real interest differentials and net foreign asset positions.[5] To see this, combine equation (1) with the familiar relative purchasing power parity equation, $\Delta s^e = \pi^e - \pi^{*e}$, where π^e is expected domestic inflation and π^{*e} is expected inflation in the rest of the world.[6] Fisher parity relates the real interest rate, r, to the nominal interest rate and expected inflation: $r = i - \pi^e$. Therefore, the real interest differential equals φ:

$$ r - r^* = (i - \pi^e) - (i^* - \pi^{*e}) = (i - i^*) - \Delta s^e = \varphi. $$

Since φ is inversely related to net foreign assets (and, in particular, to net foreign-currency assets in our theory), the real interest-rate differential is inversely related to net foreign assets.

Not only does a larger net foreign-currency asset share lead to a more negative risk premium of a creditor country, but declines in the value of domestic assets also result in a more negative risk premium. Shocks to domestic assets that lower the returns on and the market value of domestic assets result in a larger share of net foreign-currency assets. This, in turn, results in a more negative risk premium since a larger share of the portfolio is subject to foreign-exchange risk.

---

[4] Note that φ must depend upon the existence of ongoing exchange rate volatility or on the possibility of a change in the exchange rate. If neither is present, there is no foreign exchange risk.
[5] See Lane and Milesi-Ferretti (2001, Figure 11).
[6] They assume that, on average or in steady state, $q = 0$, where q is the (log of) real exchange rate.

TABLE 1
Japan's Net Foreign Asset Position, 1980–2000 (Billions of US dollars)

Year	Total Net Foreign Assets	Private Sector Net Position	Official Reserves
1980	12.52	−13.20	25.72
1985	130.38	103.15	27.23
1990	329.36	249.65	79.71
1995	817.60	632.42	184.82
1997	958.73	737.62	220.81
1998	1,153.64	937.26	215.83
1999	829.12	540.10	287.66
2000	1,157.93	796.82	360.99

Source: IMF, *International Financial Statistics* (March 2002).

Being a creditor nation, Japan has a large negative risk premium that has become more negative as it has continued to run large current account surpluses throughout the 1990s and has built up foreign currency claims on the rest of the world. Negative shocks to the Japanese economy in the late 1980s and early 1990s lowered the real return on capital in Japan relative to the rest of the world. So the Japanese invested more abroad (which was reflected in large current account surpluses) and built up claims on the rest of the world. A substantial fraction of these claims was in foreign currencies, which resulted in a more negative risk premium in the mid- to late 1990s.

In contrast, foreign currency claims on the rest of the world were small in the 1980s and domestic growth rates were high. So, the risk premium term was small, and the interest differential between dollar and yen assets was explained primarily by expectations of yen appreciation. Since the early 1990s, as Japanese growth has slowed and pressure for yen appreciation has eased, the interest differential is accounted for mainly by the negative risk premium.

Table 1 displays the rise in net foreign assets from 1980 to 2000 as reported in the International Financial Statistics (IMF, March 2002). The breakdown between official reserves and private-sector net-foreign-asset holdings is also displayed. The unit of account is billions of US dollars.

The table shows a large increase in Japan's net foreign asset position in the late 1980s and the 1990s. At the end of 2000, the total net foreign asset position stood at nearly $1.2 trillion, which is over 20 per cent of GDP or about 8 per cent of total assets.[7] A large portion of this position is held by the private sector, though accumulation of official reserves has played a large role in the late 1990s. This last point will be further examined in Section 3a.

---

[7] From the financial survey (reported in the IFS), domestic credit amounted to nearly $15 trillion in 2000.

TABLE 2

Alternate Estimates of Japan's Net Foreign Asset Position, 1980–2000 (Billions of US dollars)

Year	Official Estimate (IMF 2002)	Lane and Milesi-Ferretti (Forthcoming)	Goyal (2001) Cumulative CA Surplus	Goyal (2001) Capital Accum. (6% interest rate)
1980	12.52	16.29	12.52	12.52
1985	130.38	101.49	138.43	135.54
1990	329.36	445.96	511.39	506.99
1995	817.60	1,030.48	1,099.86	1,127.81
1997	958.73	1,336.66	1,277.93	1,337.25
2000	1,157.93		1,653.18	1,817.08

Notes:
Column 4 (Cum CA surplus) sums the balance on goods, services and income. Column 5 (Capital Accumulation) computes stocks from flow data (the balance on goods and services only) as follows:
Stock $(t) = (1 + i)$ Stock $(t - 1)$ + Flow (t).

Table 1 displays the officially reported stock of net foreign assets. Unofficial estimates of the stock position, computed by cumulating current account surpluses, suggest numbers that are about 1.5 times as large as the official statistics. Table 2 displays different estimates of Japan's cumulative current-account surplus.

The second column repeats the official net-foreign asset position from Table 1. The third column displays the cumulative current-account position from Lane and Milesi-Ferretti (2001). The fourth column updates Lane and Milesi-Ferretti's numbers to 2000. Both columns indicate numbers substantially higher than the official estimates. The final column cumulates the balance on goods and services only (the balance on income is excluded) using a six per cent yield on assets. The six per cent yield comes from Figure 2, where the return on long-term US bonds has been at least six per cent until the late 1990s. These estimates suggest that the stock of net foreign assets, and hence the external exposure of Japanese financial institutions, is very large.

The share of net foreign assets that is in foreign currencies is difficult to ascertain. Some data are available through the Bank of Japan's 'Locational International Banking Statistics,' which reports the balance sheet positions of banks and non-banks *vis-à-vis* non-residents in any currency. It is shown for selected years in Table 3.

Note that, corresponding to the increase of Japan's net foreign asset position in Tables 1 and 2, there is an increase in net assets *vis-à-vis* foreigners throughout the 1990s. A substantial portion of these net assets is in foreign currency. (Note also that the data in Table 3 are less comprehensive, and thus less in magnitude, compared to those in Tables 1 and 2.)

The breakdown of foreign assets and foreign currency assets by banks and non-banks (such as pension funds and insurance companies) is even more stark.

TABLE 3

Net Asset and Net Foreign Exchange Asset Positions of Japanese Banks and Non-banks *vis-à-vis* Non-residents, 1990–2001 (Billions of US dollars)

Year	Total		Banks		Non-Banks	
	NFA	NfxA	NFA	NfxA	NFA	NfxA
1990	−17	−101	−184	−217	167	116
1994	305	−30	87	−180	218	150
1998	477	264	103	−41	374	305
1999	612	393	142	35	470	358
2000	656	401	127	21	530	380
2001	673	449	128	34	545	415

Notes:

NFA in the title header is short for Net Foreign Assets, and *NfxA* is short for Net Foreign Exchange Assets. The numbers reported for each year correspond to the end-September number.

Source: Bank of Japan, *Locational International Banking Statistics*.

Non-banks hold the vast majority of the net foreign assets and net foreign-currency assets. A very large fraction – between 70 and 80 per cent – of their net foreign-asset positions is in foreign currency. Banks, on the other hand, borrowed heavily (in the short-term) from abroad in the 1980s. This is reflected in their net liability position in 1990. However, after making large foreign-exchange losses, they unwound much of their net short-term exposure whilst accumulating long-term foreign-currency assets.[8] Their net foreign asset and net foreign exchange asset positions are not very large.

Absent detailed balance sheet data for banks and non-banks, it is difficult to ascertain the share of net foreign-exchange assets in total assets. Balance sheet data for banks are available; however, as shown in Table 3, they are not the primary holders of net foreign and net foreign exchange assets. For non-banks such as life and non-life insurance companies, basic balance sheet data suggest that around 12 to 14 per cent of total assets are in foreign securities.[9]

The estimates of net foreign exchange assets and of exposure to foreign-exchange risk are likely to be understated. First, as noted in Table 2, unofficial net foreign-asset positions for Japanese financial institutions, estimated from simple yet meaningful computations, are nearly 1.5 times as large as official estimates. Second, balance-sheet data do not show the proportion of loans to foreigners or to multinational corporations for the purpose of foreign direct investment (FDI). Even if external FDI is denominated in yen, the investment is subject to foreign exchange risk if the proceeds of the investment or the success

---

[8] See Goyal (2001).
[9] See Bank of Japan, *Economic Statistics Annual*.

of the investment are linked to the dollar. Third, the key variable for the foreign-exchange risk premium is the share of net foreign-exchange assets to performing (or healthy) domestic assets. If a large share of total domestic assets is at risk of becoming non-performing, as is the case in Japan, then net foreign-exchange assets become a larger share of performing assets and imply a more negative foreign-exchange risk premium. As non-performing loans have ballooned in recent years, net foreign-exchange assets of nearly eight per cent of total assets become a larger share of performing assets.

So, our story is that as Japan has run current account surpluses through the 1990s and has accumulated net foreign assets and, in particular, net foreign-exchange assets, the negative risk premium has become more negative. This more negative risk premium has maintained the interest differential between yen assets and dollar assets even in the absence of trend yen appreciation. As US nominal interest rates declined due to inflation stabilisation in the United States, Japanese long rates have been compressed to very low values. Taking into account a term premium or liquidity premium, this compression of long rates has meant that short rates have been compressed to zero – a liquidity trap situation – where the Bank of Japan has been unable to halt deflation and re-inflate the economy.

This story has several implications for the Japanese banking sector. In the next section, we discuss each of these implications in turn.

3. NEGATIVE RISK PREMIUM, LOW NOMINAL INTEREST RATES AND THE BANKING SECTOR

This section is divided into three parts. The first part examines portfolio re-allocation between yen assets and foreign currency assets by private financial institutions in the liquidity trap. The second part investigates the profitability of new bank lending. The third part studies two issues regarding lending spreads and the share of bad loans in a bank's loan portfolio.

a. Portfolio Re-allocation in the Liquidity Trap

At the zero lower bound of nominal interest rates, $i = 0 = i^* + \Delta s^e + \varphi$. Recall that the left-hand side variable, i, denotes the domestic currency return on a domestic currency asset, and the right-hand side expression, $i^* + \Delta s^e + \varphi$, denotes the risk-adjusted domestic-currency return on a foreign-currency asset.

Given a portfolio allocation between foreign assets and domestic assets, and hence given a value for φ, a decline in $i^* + \Delta s^e$ due either to a decline in foreign nominal-interest rates, i^*, or to greater anticipated yen appreciation implies negative risk-adjusted domestic-currency returns on foreign-currency assets. In other words, $i = 0 > i^* + \Delta s^e + \varphi$.

Private Japanese financial institutions find it unprofitable to hold foreign-currency assets. So, they sell foreign-currency assets and buy yen assets. This portfolio re-allocation implies a less negative risk premium because exposure to foreign currency risk is reduced. However, it creates additional pressure for yen appreciation.

Yen appreciation, at a time when the Japanese economy is already quite weak, would further weaken it. To prevent this from occurring, the Japanese monetary authorities intervene in the foreign-exchange markets to sell yen and buy foreign currencies. As they do so, not only is pressure for yen appreciation alleviated (which, along with a less negative risk premium, restores interest parity at zero rates: $i = 0 = i^* + \Delta s^e + \varphi$) but also official reserve accumulation becomes the channel for dollar finance of Japan's current account surplus! For 1999 and 2000, when the nominal interest rates are zero, official reserve accumulation has indeed been the primary channel for dollar finance of the current-account surplus and for reducing what would otherwise be an even more negative currency-risk pre-mium, φ. See Table 1.[10,11]

A graphical illustration of the above argument is in Figure 4. The bold line shows interest parity above zero: $i = i^* + \Delta s^e + \varphi$. Since i is constrained below by zero, low levels of i^* (given $\Delta s^e + \varphi$) imply $i = 0 > i^* + \Delta s^e + \varphi$, where portfolio re-allocation by private Japanese financial institutions and equivalent interventions by Japanese monetary authorities result in restoration of 'parity' at a zero domestic interest rate: $i = 0 = i^* + \Delta s^e + \varphi$. However, this is a fragile equilibrium because (i) any further decline in i^*, or (ii) new foreign exchange asset accumulation from the current account surplus will lead to the same cycle of portfolio re-allocation and foreign-exchange interventions described above. After official intervention to buy dollar assets in exchange for yen assets, the equilibrium-currency-risk premium will be less negative under (i); and, under (ii), it will be prevented from becoming more negative.

In summary, in the liquidity trap with a near zero domestic interest rate, official foreign exchange interventions must continually adjust φ to maintain private portfolio balance without the yen appreciating.

b. Profitability of New Bank Lending

The compression of interest rates towards zero has an adverse impact on the profitability of new bank lending. Banks earn profits on the spread between their borrowing and lending rates. They accept various types of deposits such as demand

---

[10] Data for 2001 are not available as yet.

[11] Japan ran a current account surplus in 1999. So, a fall in its net foreign asset position in 1999 may appear puzzling. The fall is explained by a sharp increase in portfolio liabilities in 1999 associated with an inflow of foreign funds into the Japanese stock market and an increase in stock prices.

FIGURE 4
Negative Risk Premium and the Liquidity Trap

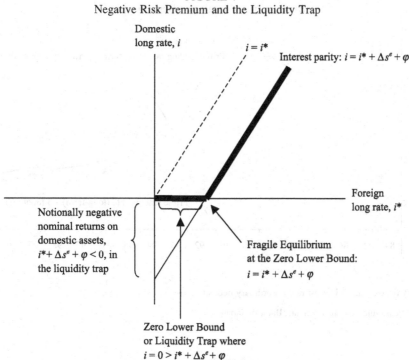

deposits at zero interest rates and time deposits, and they borrow short-term from other banks. They typically lend long-term. As the (absolute) level of lending rates falls towards zero[12] and as the spread between the short-term rates and long-term rates is compressed, banks will have very low profit margins on new loans.

Figure 5 shows the *ex-ante* profit margin on new bank lending. Two measures are plotted. One is the difference between the rate on long-term loans for prime borrowers (the prime lending rate) and the ordinary deposit rate. This measure shows a decline through the 1990s. The other measure is the difference between the prime rate on long-term loans and the three-month certificate of deposit (CD) rate, which shows an increase in the 1990s relative to the 1980s and can be explained by the deregulation of time-deposit rates.[13] Though the latter measure has increased, it remains at low levels.

Another measure of the *ex-ante* profitability of bank lending is in Figure 6, which plots the short-term and long-term rates for prime borrowers. Both rates

---

[12] Average interest rates on new loans and discounts have fallen from over 3.5 per cent before 1995 to less than 2 per cent since 1996.

[13] See Bank of Japan (2001) for an explanation of how the composition of profit margins (the sum of the lending spread and the fund-raising spread) has changed after deregulation.

FIGURE 5
Ex-Ante Profit Margins on Bank Lending

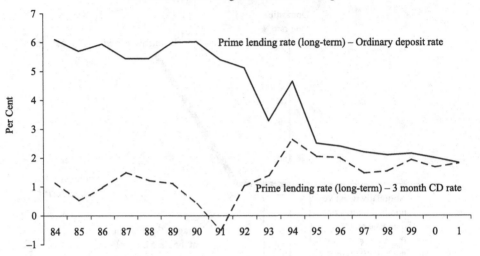

Note:
Ordinary deposit rate = interest rate on ordinary deposits.

Source: Economic Statistics Annual, Bank of Japan.

FIGURE 6
Prime Lending Rates: Short-term and Long-term

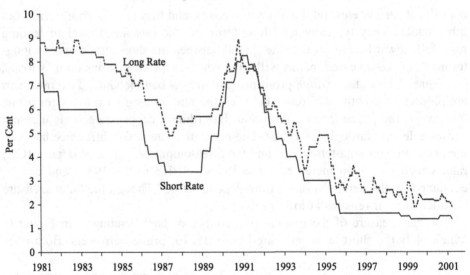

Source: Bank of Japan.

have declined in the 1990s. Significantly, the spread between the two has declined compared to the early and mid-1980s.

Though *ex-ante* measures of profitability show a decline, *ex-post* measures of profitability of bank lending do not show a similar decline unless the cost of disposing of non-performing loans is taken into account. Figure 7a plots the interest margin on lending, the cost of maintaining assets or the expense ratio, and the realised credit cost. The interest margin on lending is defined as the difference between the yield on lending and the average rate on banks' interest-bearing liabilities. The expense ratio is defined as the ratio of general and administrative expenses to the average annual balance on interest-earning assets. Realised credit costs is the ratio of loan-loss provisioning and loan write-offs (or the disposal of non-performing loans) to the average amount of loans outstanding.[14]

The interest margin on lending shows a slight decline in the 1990s. However, this decline was more than matched by a decline in general and administrative costs (or in the expense ratio). Hence, the *ex-post* interest margin on lending net of general expenses displayed in Figure 7b does not show a decline through the 1990s.

Realised credit costs or the costs associated with the disposal of non-performing loans increased dramatically in the mid- to late 1990s. Consequently, *ex-post* profitability suffered. This is displayed in Figure 7b as an interest margin on lending net of realised credit costs, and as an interest margin on lending net of realised credit costs and net of general and administrative expenses. Both measures show negative returns in the mid- to late 1990s.

How does the compression of *ex-ante* profit margins on lending square with the absence of compression in *ex-post* profit margins (not including realised credit costs)? We think it quite likely that the accounting of interest income is flawed. While Japanese banks have disposed of a large number of non-performing loans, new and larger amounts of non-performing loans keep appearing on their books. This suggests that banks have not performed adequate risk assessments of their loan portfolios, and they have not made sufficient allowances for future loan losses. It also suggests that banks may be 'evergreening' these loans and capital-ising interest payments that they have not received. The effect is that their net interest income is possibly over-stated and the reported *ex-post* net margin does not decline. But profit margins remain at very low levels.

Very low profit margins or compressed profit margins imply that Japanese banks are not earning adequate profits to cover loan losses. Comparing Japanese profit margins on lending to the margins for US banks is quite revealing. See Figure 8. US banks have been able to run much larger profit margins and,

---

[14] Data source: Bank of Japan (2001).

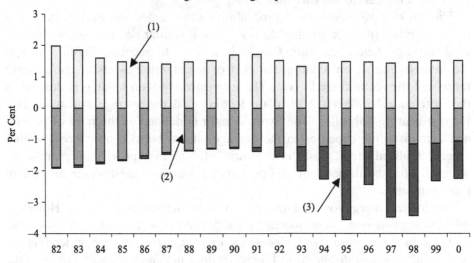

FIGURE 7a
Interest Margin on Lending, Expenses and Credit Costs

Notes:
(1) Interest margin on lending = yield on lending – average rate on banks' interest-bearing liabilities.
(2) Expense ratio = general and administrative expenses/balance on interest-earning assets.
(3) Realised credit cost = disposal of NPLs/average outstanding amount of loans.

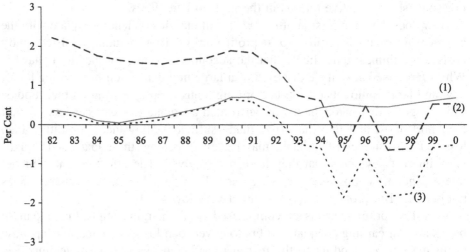

FIGURE 7b
Ex-Post Profit Margins on Bank Lending

Notes:
(1) Interest margin on lending net of general and administrative expenses.
(2) Interest margin on lending net of realised credit costs.
(3) Interest margin on lending net of general expenses and realised credit costs.

Source: Bank of Japan (2001).

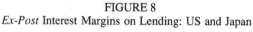

FIGURE 8
Ex-Post Interest Margins on Lending: US and Japan

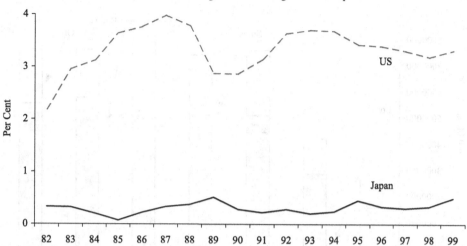

Note:
Interest margin = Yield on working assets − cost of funds.

Source: Japan: Economic Statistics Annual, Bank of Japan,
US: Comparative Economic and Financial Statistics, Bank of Japan.

thereby, have been able to cover losses on loans. Japanese banks have not been able to run as high profit margins and, hence, have been unable to cover loan losses by themselves. In the 1980s, profit margins were low because of interest-rate regulation. However, even after deregulation of the interest-rate structure, Japanese banks have been unable to generate or maintain substantially larger profit margins.

Banks may want to raise lending rates. However, they have not been able to do so to any significant degree. One possibility is that if they raise lending rates, the most credit-worthy of their corporate clients will stop borrowing from them and will instead raise credit by issuing low-yield commercial paper. This will leave banks with less credit-worthy clients. In fact, yields on newly issued commercial paper have been very low since the mid-1990s. They fell from around 2.5 per cent before 1995 to approximately 0.5 per cent since 1996, suggesting that issuers of this paper can access credit cheaply and need not pay higher interest rates to banks.[15]

Another possibility is that small and medium enterprises, who are the banks' primary clients, are already very heavily indebted and in a precarious financial situation. Raising lending rates would raise their risk of default. Bank lending shifted away from manufacturing firms in the 1980s to primarily non-manufacturing

---

[15] Data source: Bank of Japan, *Monthly Financial and Economic Statistics.*

FIGURE 9
Assets of Domestically Licensed Banks

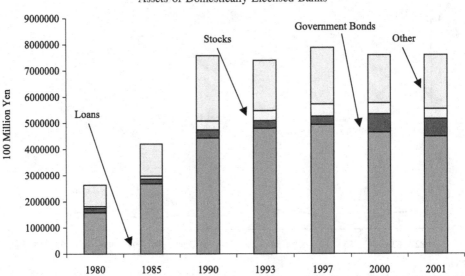

Source: Economic Statistics Annual, Bank of Japan.

firms in real estate, finance and insurance and services. In the 1990s, lending to individuals increased substantially as a share of total loans. By size of enterprise, lending has been primarily to small non-manufacturing firms.

With compressed lending rates and the zero lower bound on the deposit rates, and hence with low profit margins on new commercial lending, banks have an incentive to change their portfolio allocation away from commercial lending and into low-transaction-cost government bonds. This is indeed what has happened in Japan. Loans outstanding have declined from the mid-1990s while the amount of government bonds has increased quite substantially. See Figure 9. Bank credit to the private sector has been shrinking in the late 1990s, as shown in Figure 1, even though the monetary base and broad money (M2 + CDs) have been increasing.

c. Low Lending Spreads and the Share of Bad Loans in a Bank's Portfolio

Compressed lending rates and low profit margins have made it practically impossible for Japanese banks, by themselves, to cover loan losses and gradually write off old bad loans out of current earnings. By contrast, US banks have been able to gradually recover loan losses because their profit margins on lending have been much larger than has been possible for Japanese banks. See Figure 8.

This section presents two simple exercises to show the relationship between lending spreads and the share of non-performing loans in a bank's portfolio. First, the lending spread required to recover a given share of non-performing loans in T periods of time is computed. Second, given a particular lending spread, the evolution of the size of loanable funds is studied.

Consider a simple model of a bank. The bank has a given level of deposits and has made loans. Assume that a share of the loans has become non-performing. Assume further that the non-performing loans (NPLs) are maintained on the balance sheet of the bank, that is, the non-performing loans are not immediately written-off. And suppose that no new funds come to the bank: there is neither a public injection of funds nor new deposits.

If the bank is to cover its loan losses, it needs to do so out of current profits. Given an initial NPL share, in how much time can the bank cover its loan losses as a function of the lending spread?

The balance sheet of the bank may be described as follows:

Assets	Liabilities
Loans	Deposits
NPLs	Capital
Performing Loans	
Reserves	

Let i_l be the lending rate, let i_d be the deposit rate, and let τ be the general and administrative cost per unit of assets. Let k be the capital adequacy ratio and let r be the required reserve ratio. Let total liabilities be normalised to 1, and let the share of NPLs at time t be NPA_t.

Assuming no new defaults, the bank's revenue per yen lent at time t is $i_l(1 - r - NPA_t)$. Its cost at time t is $i_d(1 - k) + \tau$. Hence, its profit rate at time t, π_t, is given by:

$$\pi_t = i_l(1 - r - NPA_t) - i_d(1 - k) - \tau. \tag{2}$$

Assume that (positive) profits are used to write off loan losses. The evolution of the non-performing loan share is given by:

$$NPA_{t+1} = NPA_t - \pi_t. \tag{3}$$

Given an initial share of non-performing loans, NPA_0, and given i_d, τ, k and r, we can compute the time to cover loan losses as a function of the lending rate, i_l. We do so by setting $NPA_T = 0$ and iterating backwards using equations (2) and (3). See the Appendix for details.

Let $i_d = 0$, $\tau = 1.5$ per cent, $k = 10$ per cent and $r = 2$ per cent. This parametrisation roughly corresponds to the situation of Japanese banks.

Figure 10 displays the time taken to reduce the share of non-performing loans in the bank's balance sheet to zero as a function of the lending rate i_l (given a

FIGURE 10
Time to Cover Loan Losses for a Given Initial Non-performing Asset Share
(Assuming Zero Deposit Rate): A Simulation

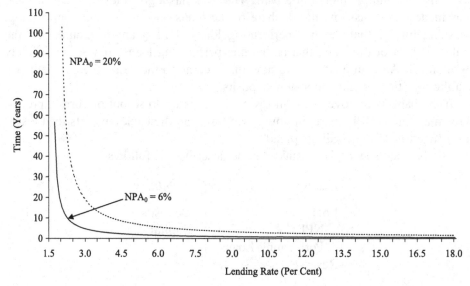

zero deposit rate). As one would expect, the lower the lending spread, the longer it takes to cover loan losses. The larger the initial share of non-performing assets, the longer it takes to cover loan losses. The time taken to cover loan losses increases exponentially as the lending spread declines.

By official estimates, the share of non-performing loans is 6 per cent.[16] From Figure 5, the *ex-ante* profit margins are approximately 1.7 per cent. Given a spread of 1.7 per cent, it will take over 56 years to cover the loan losses. This computation assumes no new defaults and no infusion of funds. If there is a continuing risk of default, as there most likely will be, then this is an under-estimate and it will take longer to cover the losses. Furthermore, in the past ten years, there has been little change in the total deposit base of domestically licensed banks. There have been public infusions of funds, but these have been few and in times of (near) crisis.

Unofficial estimates of the share of non-performing loans are as high as 20 per cent. For such high loan losses, it would take over 100 years to recover losses at a spread of 2 per cent. For spreads lower than 1.9 per cent, the banks are running at a loss and are unable to cover their loan losses. Indeed, the spreads required for Japanese banks to make profits and cover losses are much larger than they have been able to generate. Figure 6 is also suggestive of their troubles since the

---

[16] See Bank of Japan (2001).

spread between the short-term rate and long-term rate has been about 0.5 per cent, which is far smaller than the spreads that they need to restore financial health.

The exercise strongly suggests that low lending spreads are a key component of the problems faced by Japanese banks. Lowering τ and lowering r would reduce the lending spreads needed to cover loan losses and, in fact, Japanese banks have been trying to lower τ by reducing personnel expenses. Reducing τ and r in the computations reduces the time needed to cover loan losses; however, the time needed remains high. For a 20 per cent initial share of non-performing loans and for τ reduced to 1 per cent and r reduced to 1 per cent, 40 years are needed to cover loan losses for a lending spread of 1.7 per cent. For a 6 per cent share, the time is ten years. This computation assumes no defaults on new loans.

A spread of over 3 per cent, which US banks have been able to generate, implies that a 6 per cent initial non-performing loan share can be covered in less than five years at the initial parametrisation. After the savings and loan crisis of the late 1980s and early 1990s, the ratio of non-performing loans rose significantly in the portfolio of US banks. However, they were not very high and, with spreads over 3 per cent, US banks have easily recovered their losses. With larger non-performing loans and smaller lending spreads, Japanese banks on the other hand face a much more difficult time in covering their losses.

With low lending spreads and large non-performing loans, the computations suggest that Japanese banks are losing money on their operations. What is the impact on bank lending if the banks are unable to break even?

In our simple model, if $\pi_t < 0$ and the bank makes losses, then its capital (or net worth) declines. To maintain a required level of capital, the bank must call in, or not renew, some of its performing (or good) loans to reduce its liabilities. As performing loans are called in, non-performing assets rise as a share of performing assets. That is, the 'loan dependency ratio' of non-performing loans to performing loans worsens over time even if there are no new defaults!

We have computed and plotted this 'loan dependency ratio' over time for the case of an initial non-performing asset share of 20 per cent. Let total liabilities be normalised initially, that is, at time 0, to 1. Hence, non-performing assets at time 0 are 0.20. As in the exercise above, let the required reserve ratio be 2 per cent and let the capital adequacy ratio be 10 per cent of total liabilities. Let the lending rate i_l be 1.7 per cent, let the deposit rate i_d be 0 per cent and let the general and administrative expense ratio τ be 1.5 per cent.

Figure 11 plots the exponential increase in the ratio of non-performing assets to performing assets over time. The ratio increases gradually at first, rising from 26 per cent at time 0 (corresponding to non-performing assets as a 20 per cent share of total liabilities at time 0) to 29 per cent in five years and 34 per cent after ten years. After that, the increases are much quicker. So, the bad loan problem can fester for some years before it explodes.

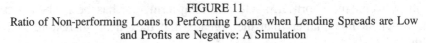

FIGURE 11

Ratio of Non-performing Loans to Performing Loans when Lending Spreads are Low
and Profits are Negative: A Simulation

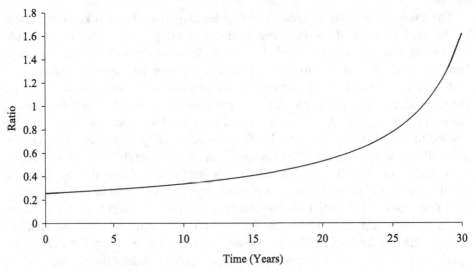

d. Public Financial Intermediation

An alternative interpretation, put forth by Fukao (2002), is that profit margins
are low not because of pressure coming in from the foreign exchange market, as
we have argued, but in large part because government financial institutions have
been providing funds at low interest rates, thus keeping commercial loan rates
low. But, the question is one of causality or endogeneity. Is public intermediation
driving the non-profitability of commercial bank lending or is public intermediation an endogenous response to a curtailment in (unprofitable) commercial bank
lending? Fukao suggests the former, but we suspect that it may be the latter.

Figure 12 plots the prime long-term lending rate, the key lending rates of
government financial institutions and the Fiscal Loan Fund. The key lending
rates of the government financial institutions move very closely with the prime
long-term lending rate. The two are virtually identical for many periods. They
also move very closely with the Fiscal Loan Fund rate, and have declined
significantly over the 1990s. While the co-movement and the fall are apparent
throughout the 1990s, the causality from one to the other is not.

Figure 13 plots the prime long-term lending rate with the middle rates on
housing loans by City Banks and the lending rates on private dwellings by the
Housing Loan Corporation. The loan rates of City Banks have moved nearly
identically with the prime long-term rates and, since 1995, have been below
the rates offered by the Housing Loan Corporation. Housing loan rates of the

FIGURE 12

Lending Rates: Prime Rates, Government Financial Institutions Rates and Fiscal Loan Funds Rate and Fiscal Loan Funds Rate, 1989–2001

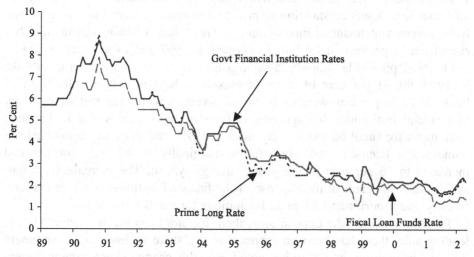

Source: Financial and Economic Statistics Monthly, Bank of Japan.

FIGURE 13

Housing Loan Rates: City Banks (Middle Rate) and Housing Loan Corporation

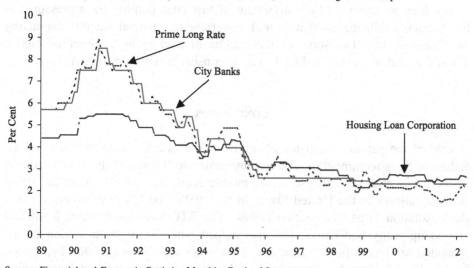

Source: Financial and Economic Statistics Monthly, Bank of Japan.

latter have declined in the 1990s, but it does not appear that the Housing Loan Corporation is undercutting the profit margins of commercial bank lending.

On the loan side, commercial bank credit to private non-financial corporations has fallen in absolute terms since 1996–97. As argued above, commercial banks have instead increased their holdings of government securities. Loans from government financial institutions to private non-financial corporations rose in the early 1990s but have fallen in absolute terms since 1998. In relative terms, a slightly larger share of loans outstanding to private non-financial corporations has come from government financial intermediaries. Their share of loans outstanding has risen from 11 per cent in 1990 to 13 per cent in 1997 and 14 per cent in 2000.[17]

On the deposit side, household savings have increased throughout the 1990s. In 1989–90, 41 per cent of these savings were held in domestically licensed banks while 31 per cent were in the postal savings system. The rest were mostly in financial institutions for agriculture, forestry and fisheries and in financial institutions for small businesses. By the late 1990s, the share of savings held in domestically licensed banks had fallen marginally to 40 per cent but had increased to 36 per cent in the postal-savings system. The increase in postal-savings deposits came at the expense of the financial institutions for agriculture, forestry and fisheries and financial institutions for small businesses.

To summarise, on the deposit side, there has not been much change. On the lending side, there has been an increase in the share of loans by government financial institutions, as Fukao has noted. But, this change is not large and there does not appear to be much evidence of undercutting of private lending rates by government financial institutions. Nevertheless, the evidence of government financial institutions offering low rates and increasing lending to the private sector does not contradict our argument of low rates coming from pressures in the foreign exchange market – and government financial institutions acting endogenously to offset some of the decline in lending by commercial banks. Thus, the evidence presented by Fukao is consistent with our explanation.

4. CONCLUSION

One of the supposed truisms about Japan's economic malaise has been the failure of the government to take resolute action to 'clean up' the balance sheets of the banks after the collapse of the bubble economy in 1991. After the string of bank failures in the United States in the 1980s, the US government created the Resolution Trust Corporation (1989). The RTC assumed dubious loans and wound up really bad banks, but also helped with the re-capitalisation of the wounded survivors often by subsidising a merger with, or acquisition by, a good bank. Although there have been several desultory attempts to inject more capital into distressed (and not so distressed!) Japanese banks, nothing seems to work to stem the fall in new bank credit. Thus, with invidious comparisons to the earlier

---

[17] Data source: Bank of Japan.

American example, the Japanese government is heavily criticised for not being thorough enough in restructuring commercial and other domestic banks.

However, our analysis of the negative risk premium and Japan's low-interest rate trap suggests that such criticism of government regulatory inaction is seriously misplaced. Instead, macroeconomic phenomena have compressed bank lending (as well as deposit) rates toward zero so as to take away the 'normal' margin of profitability on new lending. This compressed margin helps explain both the reluctance of Japanese banks to make new loans and their inability to gradually re-capitalise themselves. In contrast, after the banking crises of the 1980s, most US banks could gradually re-capitalise because the spread between deposit and loan rates for several years was even higher than it is now – and much higher than in Japan currently.

A comprehensive restructuring of balance sheets, no matter how thorough, cannot end Japan's banking crisis. Under the currently compressed structure of interest rates on yen assets, commercial banks will remain reluctant to lend to high-quality borrowers. Decompression and a return to a more normal structure of nominal interest rates through macroeconomic reforms should precede serious balance sheet restructuring, which of course will ultimately be necessary.

Thus, ending the low-interest liquidity trap is a necessary condition for the recovery of Japan's banking system. If one accepts our hypothesis of the importance of the negative risk premium in contributing to Japan's low-interest rate trap, then what should be done is obvious. The negative risk premium arises from: (1) decades of accumulation of dollar assets within Japanese financial institutions; and (2) fluctuations in the yen/dollar exchange rate, which increase the risks to yen-based financial firms from holding these dollar assets. Because running trade deficits cannot suddenly reverse the cumulative financial effect of 20 years of trade surpluses, the only immediate policy instrument for reducing the foreign exchange risk in Japanese financial intermediaries is to stabilise the yen/dollar exchange rate in a completely convincing fashion.

How to credibly stabilise the yen/dollar rate into the indefinite future, and the macroeconomic consequences of doing so, is a story for another time (McKinnon and Ohno, 1997 and 2001; and Goyal, 2001). Here it suffices to note that the solution, as well as the problem, is not one that the Japanese authorities are likely to be able to deal with on their own. Rather, to be credible, a long-term benchmark parity for the yen/dollar rate will require the full cooperation of the United States.

APPENDIX

a. Case of Positive Operational Profits: $\pi_t > 0$

Combining equations (2) and (3) yields:

$$\text{NPA}_T = (1 + i_l)\text{NPA}_{T-1} - i_l(1 - r) + i_d(1 - k) + \tau.$$

Iterating backwards to time 0 gives:

$$\text{NPA}_T = (1 + i_l)^T\text{NPA}_0 - [i_l(1 - r) + i_d(1 - k) + \tau][1 + (1 + i_l) \\ + (1 + i_l)^2 + \cdots + (1 + i_l)^{T-1}].$$

This equation can be used to compute the time T needed to cover loan losses of NPA_0 given i_l, i_d, τ, k and r. This is done by setting $\text{NPA}_T = 0$. The equation then reduces to:

$$i_l\text{NPA}_0 = [1 - (1 + i_l)^{-T}][i_l(1 - r) + i_d(1 - k) + \tau].$$

It can be solved for T. Alternatively, the equation can be used to determine the lending rate i_l needed to cover initial loan losses NPA_0 for a given time period of, say, ten years.

b. Case of Negative Operational Profits: $\pi_t < 0$

Losses erode bank capital. Let k_t be bank capital at time t. Since losses erode capital:

$$k_{t+1} = k_t + \pi_t < k_t.$$

Banks must maintain a certain capital adequacy ratio, denoted by k^*. So, its liabilities, which are deposits D_t, must shrink. Deposits must shrink such that $k_{t+1}/(k_{t+1} + D_{t+1}) = k^*$. Thus, the size of the bank $(k_{t+1} + D_{t+1})$ shrinks.

As liabilities shrink, so do required reserves and, more importantly, the performing assets. Performing loans are called in or are not renewed. Hence, non-performing loans rise as a share of performing loans.

REFERENCES

Bank of Japan (2001), 'Developments in Profits and Balance Sheets of Japanese Banks in Fiscal 2000 and Banks' Management Tasks,' *Bank of Japan Quarterly Bulletin* **9**, 4 (November), 73–130.
Bank of Japan (2002), *Locational International Banking Statistics* (http://www.boj.or.jp/en/).
Fukao, M. (2002), 'Japan's Lost Decade and Weaknesses in its Corporate Governance Structure,' Paper presented at the Symposium, Japan's Lost Decade: Origins, Consequences and Prospects for Recovery (University of Michigan (March); a revised version is included in this Symposium).
Goyal, R. (2001), 'Foreign Exchange Risk and Japan's Liquidity Trap' (Stanford University, mimeo).
International Monetary Fund (2002), *International Financial Statistics*, CD-ROM (March).

Krugman, P. (1998), 'It's Baaack: Japan's Slump and the Return of the Liquidity Trap,' *Brookings Papers on Economic Activity*, **2**, 137–87.

Lane, P. and G. M. Milesi-Ferretti (2001), 'Long-Term Capital Movements,' *NBER Macroeconomics Annual 2001* (Cambridge: MIT Press).

McKinnon, R. I. and K. Ohno (1997), *Dollar and Yen: Resolving Economic Conflict between the United States and Japan* (Cambridge: MIT Press).

McKinnon, R. I. and K. Ohno (2001), 'The Foreign Exchange Origins of Japan's Economic Slump and Low Interest Liquidity Trap,' *The World Economy*, **24**, 279–315.

Shirakawa, M. (2001), 'Monetary Policy Under the Zero Interest Rate Constraint and Balance Sheet Adjustment,' *International Finance*, **4**, 463–89.

Svensson, L. (2001), 'The Zero Bound in an Open Economy: A Foolproof Way of Escaping from a Liquidity Trap,' *Monetary and Economic Studies*, Special Edition (Institute for Monetary and Economic Studies, Bank of Japan), **19**, S-1, 277–312.

Yoshikawa, H. (1990), 'On the Equilibrium Yen-Dollar Rate,' *American Economic Review*, **80**, 576–83.

6

Japan's Lost Decade and its Financial System

Mitsuhiro Fukao

1. INTRODUCTION

AFTER the collapse of the bubble, most of the unrealised profit in holdings of stock and real estate has disappeared. Banks have used up their unrealised capital gains to cover loan losses. Banks and life-insurance companies no longer have the equity buffer necessary for maintaining very large stock portfolios for cross-shareholding purposes.

The Government used to have a 'pocket' to use at its discretion. The regulatory rent in the financial sector derived from the deposit interest and branching controls was used to take care of failed financial institutions. Even if a failed bank had a negative equity, Ministry of Finance (MOF) officials could easily find a healthy bank for a merger. The Fiscal Investment and Loan Programme (FILP) also relied on this rent. The Government-sponsored financial institutions (GSFIs) could distribute a part of a large gap between the regulated deposit interest rate and the on-going lending rate as a subsidy to the preferred borrower. Even if a FILP finance project went sour, the Government could provide implicit subsidies with low interest loans.

By phasing out deposit interest and branching controls in the late 1980s and early 1990s, MOF officials lost power to give credible commitment to the private financial institutions. In order to take care of bank failures, MOF officials now have to obtain an explicit budget allocation. The extremely strong public resistance to the use of what now appears a very small amount of public money (0.685 trillion yen), to solve the *jusen* problem in 1996 forced the MOF to postpone the resolution of the bad loan problem of the banking sector.

MITSUHIRO FUKAO is from Keio University. He would like to thank Mariko Sakakibara, E. Han Kim and other Symposium participants for helpful comments.

GSFIs also need taxpayers' money to provide low interest loans. However, the subsidised loans by GSFIs have made it extremely difficult for banks to earn a profit because they also lost rent from deposit-interest controls. Under the current deflationary economic environment with large debt overhangs among borrowers, banks cannot cover the cost of loan losses with their thin profit margins. In order to resolve the bad-loan problem in the banking sector, banks have to raise lending interest rates to their main customers, i.e., small and medium sized firms.

On the other hand, small and medium sized firms are also on the losing side. They used to receive at least a part of the regulatory rent from the banking sector as relatively low interest rates on their debt. Using the short-term money market rate as a benchmark, they are now paying about two percentage points more on their bank borrowing than they used to pay in the 1980s. As a result, the real borrowing cost of smaller companies remains relatively high in spite of the zero-interest policy of the Bank of Japan. Thus, most small and medium sized firms cannot readily afford to pay higher interest rates to banks. Probably, the only way out from this impasse is a mild inflation. If the Bank of Japan could stop deflation with strong monetary expansion, it would be possible to have a higher nominal lending interest rate and a lower real borrowing rate.

2. THE REAL ESTATE BUBBLE AND FINANCIAL CRISIS

In this section, I briefly review the process of the asset price bubble and the developments of the financial crisis in the 1990s.

a. The Origin of the Problem

In order to examine the origin of Japan's financial problems, let us briefly review the magnitude of the Japanese asset price bubble in the 1980s. The market value of the Tokyo Stock Exchange 1st Section as a ratio to nominal GDP had remained in the 20–40 per cent range from the early 1950s to the early 1980s. However, stock prices started to rise in the mid-1980s and reached 150 per cent by the end of 1989. After the crash of the bubble, this ratio fell to about the 50–70 per cent range. In relation to nominal GDP, residential land prices almost doubled in the second half of the 1980s, and the commercial land prices tripled in the same period. After the bubble, the fall of the commercial land price index was extremely sharp. It fell to only 20 per cent of the peak level relative to nominal GDP.

The asset price bubble was created by the following three factors: loose monetary policy; tax distortions; and financial deregulation.[1] In countries where these three factors were in place, asset price inflation was often observed. In this respect, the Japanese

---

[1] See Shigemi (1995) and BIS (1993) on the causes of asset price inflation in major countries.

case was not an abnormal phenomenon. However, the magnitude of the asset-price bubble in Japan was enormous and the impact of its collapse was extremely severe.

(i) Easy monetary policy

Japanese monetary policy in the late 1980s was clearly too loose. Policy makers put too much weight on stabilising the appreciating yen and too little weight on stabilising the asset price bubble and the overheating economy. The Bank of Japan (BOJ) tried to tighten monetary policy in late 1987 so as to counter the overheating economy and rising asset prices. However, the sharp fall in stock prices on Black Monday in the United States in October prevented this move. The BOJ did not raise its discount rate until May 1989, and it failed to stop the asset-price bubble at an early stage. Stock prices defied the intention of the BOJ and continued to rise until the end of 1989. Land prices hit their peak in early 1990. If the BOJ had acted in late 1987, it could have alleviated the severity of asset price deflation in the 1990s.

(ii) Tax distortions

The Japanese tax system favoured debt financed real estate investment until the end of *the bubble*, as the following examples illustrate.

1. The marginal rate of inheritance tax has been very high in Japan. It was 75 per cent over 500 million yen until 1988, and it is still 70 per cent over 2 billion yen. However, the evaluation of land for taxation used to be about one half of the market value, and the debt was evaluated at its face value during the bubble period. As a result, wealthy individuals borrowed money to buy land so as to reduce the inheritance tax.
2. Capital gains on land were not taxed until the time of its sale, and interest payments can be deducted from taxable income for companies and for those individuals who are investing in condominiums and offices. Moreover, the effective property tax rate on land was very low, about 0.1 per cent of the market value, until the early 1990s. As a result, a large number of real estate investments were carried out for tax planning purposes.

(iii) Financial deregulations

The financial system in Japan was liberalised very gradually. The driving forces behind this liberalisation process were the massive issuance of government bonds in the late 1970s and the increasing internationalisation of financial markets. Ceilings on bank deposit interest rates were liberalised gradually from large-denomination to smaller ones from 1985 to 1994. Restrictions on the issuance of corporate bonds were gradually liberalised during the 1980s. As a result, large listed companies, which are traditional customers of Japanese banks, gradually shifted their funding from banks to the capital market. Banks faced a prospect of profit squeeze due to rising funding costs and a declining customer base.

In view of the declining rent from the traditional business of retail deposit taking and commercial lending to large firms, banks tried to increase their middle-market business. Most banks started to increase real estate lending. In expanding such lending, banks exclusively relied on collateral and paid little attention to the cash flow of underlying business. This was because the nominal land price in Japan had been on a rising trend since the end of World War II, and the pace of land-price inflation was higher than government bond interest rates on average. This land-price performance created a general perception by bankers that they could always avoid loan losses so long as loans were secured by real estate. This was certainly true until the collapse of *the bubble* in the 1990s. Many banks solicited loans to customers by providing information on real-estate-investment opportunities. During *the bubble* period, even an ordinary salaried worker living in Tokyo could easily borrow up to 100 million yen for any purpose at the long-term prime rate if his house could be used as collateral. Thus, financial liberalisation created a perfect environment for an asset-price bubble where firms and households could easily acquire real estate with borrowed money in the 1980s.

Financial intermediation by banks expanded significantly in the 1980s. The bank lending-GDP ratio rose from 70 per cent of GDP in the late 1970s to 108 per cent by 1990. The composition of the loan portfolios of Japanese banks also changed dramatically. The share of the manufacturing sector in the loan portfolio declined from 25 per cent in 1977 to less than 15 per cent by the end of the 1980s. On the other hand, the share of loans to real estate and financing companies rose sharply in the same period. Since lending to financing companies such as *jusen* (housing loan companies) was meant for real estate investment, the involvement of banks in real-estate-related lending was very large in the 1980s.

b. Slow-moving Financial Crisis: 1991–96

(i) Increasing problem loans

Reflecting a successive tightening of monetary policy from May 1989 until February 1991, stock and real estate prices started to decline rapidly. The ratio of the land price index to nominal GDP had declined twice in the previous 30 years. In the early 1970s when the ratio declined, the nominal land price did not decline much and this fall was induced by a sharp inflation of the prices of goods and services. However, in the 1990s, the fall in this ratio was induced by a fall in nominal land prices. These differences are important in evaluating the fallout from the collapse of *the bubble*. In the first episode, investors who bought land with borrowed money could repay their debt. On the other hand, in the second episode, real estate investors could not honour their debt obligations.

At first, bankers and bank supervisors thought that the fall in land prices would be temporary. They expected that by waiting for a recovery of the economy, banks could eventually recover most of their bad loans. However, the wait-and-see strategy did not work this time, and real estate prices continued to fall. In order to avoid dealing with their bad-loan problems, some banks turned to falsification of their financial statements. Since falsification of financial statements of listed companies carried a stiff criminal penalty, the management of banks with large bad loans faced a difficult choice, that is, covering up the extent of their problem to keep their bank open or face a bank run by disclosing the reality. They typically chose the first option. Apparently, bank supervisors actively supported this choice of option until early 1997. It was under the heavy pressure of public opinion for a transparent resolution of the financial crisis that the disclosure of problem loans was gradually expanded.

(ii) Declining credit ratings and Japan premium

Reflecting the increasing loan losses and declining stock prices, the credit rating of Japanese banks declined rapidly. In the mid-1980s, Japanese banks enjoyed their highest credit ratings under regulated interest rates and huge unrealised capital gains in their equity portfolio. However, financial deregulation and asset-price deflation completely changed the relative creditworthiness of Japanese banks. By 1992, Japanese banks had the lowest average credit rating among major countries.

Against this dire picture, both the Ministry of Finance (MOF) and the Bank of Japan (BOJ) denied the severity of the bad-loan problem and collaborated to postpone the costly resolution of insolvent financial institutions. There are several reasons for the slow response of policy makers.

1. A number of large financial institutions were either insolvent or severely undercapitalised.
2. In order to resolve the crisis, public money was needed. However, using taxpayers' money was not popular.
3. High officials of the Banking Bureau of the MOF rotate every few years. As a result, there was a strong incentive for them to postpone the resolution of politically difficult problems.

One important factor in this context was the mismanagement of the *jusen* crisis. *Jusen* companies are non-bank financial institutions, and they were affiliates of groups of banks. *Jusen* started their business as housing-loan companies, but their business was limited by two factors. The Japan Housing Loan Corporation, a governmental loan company, provided subsidised loans with prime collateral. Parent banks also started to provide housing loans in the late 1970s. As a result, the *jusen* companies were gradually marginalised in the housing loan market. In the 1980s, *jusen* companies then started to shift their business to riskier real estate loans, and they often took second-rated collateral to make high-risk loans.

After the collapse of *the bubble*, *jusen* companies quickly became insolvent. This became obvious for related parties by 1992–93, but parent banks and MOF officials decided to wait for a recovery of real estate prices. By 1995, it had become a serious political problem. Since *jusen* companies financed their real estate loans with borrowed money from small agricultural credit unions, the failure of *jusen* companies could induce failures of a number of such credit unions. Since agricultural credit unions had a strong lobby in the Diet, the national congress of Japan, politicians put strong pressure on the MOF to resolve the *jusen* crisis without inducing the failures of agricultural credit unions. As a result, 680 billion yen of public money was used to cover a part of the losses of the credit unions without bankruptcy procedures or asking the managers to take responsibility. All but one *jusen* companies were liquidated and most of the losses were borne by parent banks. Against this rather skewed scheme of *jusen* resolution developed by the MOF and politicians, public opinion was extremely critical, making it politically impossible to discuss further use of public money to resolve the financial crisis. As a result, there was a further postponement of the resolution of the crisis.

Market participants were well aware of Japan's problem. As the asset-price deflation continued, the funding cost of Japanese banks started to increase relative to European and American banks due to the rising credit-risk of Japanese banks. Even the soundest banks had to pay a risk premium (the so-called Japan premium) for their inter-bank borrowings.

c. The Japanese Financial Crisis since 1997

In November 1997, the failure of Sanyo Securities, Hokkaido Takushoku Bank, and Yamaichi Securities sharply increased financial instability. These events generated a severe credit crunch in the Japanese financial market, inducing an extremely serious recession. In my judgment, there were two factors responsible for this crisis.

One is the crash of the stock and real estate market bubble in the 1990s. The second is the lost confidence in the accounting and auditing system in Japan. It appears that the actual amount of bad loans discovered at failed financial institutions was far larger than the amount published prior to failure. The Hokkaido Takushoku Bank was forced into bankruptcy even though it posted profits and paid dividends for the year to March 1997. Financial statements for that year reported 0.3 trillion yen in capital; inspections after the failure found a negative equity of 1.2 trillion yen as of 31 March, 1998. This indicates window-dressing of almost 1.5 trillion yen.

Likewise, Yamaichi Securities was hiding 260 billion yen of losses on securities investments – worth more than one-half of its equity capital – which neither MOF inspections nor BOJ examinations were reportedly able to uncover.

Depositors and investors in bank debentures issued by long-term credit banks imposed some market discipline. Deposits were withdrawn from banks with low credit ratings because depositors feared that they would not be able to withdraw their deposits quickly if the banks were closed. The Long-Term Credit Bank of Japan and Nippon Credit Banks faced an acceleration in the early redemption of their debentures because such debentures were not covered explicitly by the deposit insurance system. Stock prices of weaker banks fell sharply and triggered mild bank runs in some cases.

These financial-institution failures exacerbated suspicions both at home and abroad regarding the financial statements and regulatory supervision of Japanese financial institutions. It was this mistrust of financial statements that widened the 'Japan premium' charged in overseas markets, blocked the domestic call market (which is used for short-term inter-bank loans), and multiplied the number of cash-pressed financial institutions turning to the BOJ for loans. Japanese financial markets clearly experienced a kind of credit crunch because of a rash of failures, declining asset prices, and growing mistrust of financial statements and regulators. This credit crunch in turn cut into corporate investment and hiring, increased bankruptcy rates, and reduced consumption and housing investments because workers feared losing their jobs. The result was a further contraction of credit in what became a vicious cycle. In other words, unreliable financial statements had proved a serious impediment to the functioning of a market economy.

The contraction was somewhat abated by the Emergency Economic Package announced by the Liberal Democratic Party and MOF at the end of 1997. The Government provided 13 trillion yen for a capital injection to solvent banks and 17 trillion yen for the protection of depositors of failed banks. The MOF should have used the funds more effectively. By forcing banks to write off all the bad loans, the financial institutions and the financial oversight by the government could have regained public confidence. However, instead, most of the money was left unused. Only 1.8 trillion yen of 13 trillion yen was thinly injected in 21 large banks at the end of March 1998 without any complete examination or comprehensive clean-up of bank balance sheets.

The failure of the capital injection became apparent only a few months later. In the summer of 1998, the stock price of the Long-Term Credit Bank of Japan (LTCB) fell sharply when the Sumitomo Trust and Banking effectively refused a merger with the LTCB. The LTCB was a large bank with 26.2 trillion yen of assets at the end of March 1998. In October 1998, just before the LTCB went bankrupt, the Financial Revitalisation Act and Bank Recapitalisation Act were enacted in a disorderly atmosphere. This time, the Government provided 60 trillion yen, about 12 per cent of GDP. There was provision of 25 trillion yen for the capital injection into solvent banks under the Bank Recapitalisation Act, 18 trillion yen for the resolution of failing banks under the Financial Revitalisation Act for rescue banks, bridge banks, and the disposition of bad loans, and 17 trillion yen for the protection of depositors by the Deposit Insurance Corporation.[2]

Under the Financial Revitalisation Act, the LTCB and Nippon Credit Bank were nationalised in October and December 1998. Under the Bank Recapitalisation Act, 7.5 trillion yen of capital was injected into 15 major banks at the end of

---

[2] See Fukao (2000) for the detail of the Bank Recapitalisation Act and Financial Revitalisation Act.

March 1999. Unlike the former attempt, this programme was much better designed and succeeded in eliminating the persistent Japan premium that had arisen in late 1997. The gradual recovery of the Japanese economy and the announcements of big mergers among major banks have also contributed to calm the public concern over the financial system.

However, the total net cost of these measures will not be known for years to come because the Government may recover some of these costs by the sales of bad loans and bank stocks. Gross cost of these operations from 1992 until the summer of 2000 is about 27 trillion yen and can be broken down as follows:[3]

Cost of Capital Injection: 10 trillion yen
Cost of Grant to Buyer of Failed Institutions   13 trillion yen
Cost of Purchasing Bad Loans   4 trillion yen.

In May 2000, the Deposit Insurance Law was amended so as to prepare a permanent resolution scheme for failing banks because the Financial Revitalisation Act and Bank Recapitalisation Act was to expire at the end of March 2001. In this amendment, a bridge-bank scheme and a procedure of systemic exception from the minimum cost principle became a permanent feature of the system. The introduction of the application of a 10 million yen cap on the deposit-insurance coverage for time deposits was postponed for one year from the end of March 2001. Moreover, the full protection of demand deposits was extended until the end of March 2003. Ten trillion yen was added to the 17 trillion yen fund for the protection of depositors.

3. WEAK JAPANESE BANKING SYSTEM

Since the sharp decline of asset prices in 1990, more than a decade has passed. The acute financial crisis in 1998 abated more than three years ago. However, Japan is still facing an increasing amount of bad loans and a very fragile economy.[4]

a. The Bad-loan Situation in Japan

Japanese banks have lost 75 trillion yen due to bad loans from March 1992 until September 2001. In spite of this enormous loss that amounted to 15 per cent

---

[3] See Horie (2001).
[4] In addition to the weak banking system, there is a need to stabilise life insurance companies, exemplified by the recent failure of Chiyoda, Kyoei and Tokyo Life Insurance. Life insurance policies are an important saving instrument in Japan and this sector controls more than 200 trillion yen of assets. Life insurance companies promised high minimum returns on their long-lasting life insurance and annuity policies in the 1980s and early 1990s. But since they did not match the duration of their assets and liabilities, they faced an enormous negative yield gap when Japan experienced very low nominal interest rates in the late 1990s. For a more detailed discussion, see Fukao and Japan Centre for Economic Research (2000b).

of GDP in 2000, Japanese banks still have 36 trillion yen of disclosed bad loans or about 7 per cent of their loan portfolios at the end of September 2001. According to the Financial Services Agency, the total classified loans of banks (not disclosed on an individual basis) amounted to 68 trillion yen. The classified loans are more than twice as much as the disclosed bad-loan total.

While the bad-loan/total loan ratio has stabilised for city banks, the ratio for first-tier and second-tier regional banks has been increasing rapidly. This is partly due to the application of a tougher classification standard by the FSA and also is due to the deteriorating loan quality for smaller financial institutions.

The cause of this increasing amount of bad loans without loan-loss reserves is the low profitability of the Japanese banking sector. Since banks do not earn enough profit to write off all the bad loans, they try to postpone the recognition of losses so as to show a relatively favourable capital position. If they write off bad loans immediately, most banks would not be able to comply with the Bank for International Settlements (BIS) capital requirements and they may even have to show a negative equity position.

b. Bank Profitability

Table 1 shows the profit structure of the Japanese banking sector. The gross lending margin (A), which is the difference between interest and dividend income received and the interest paid, has been about 10 trillion yen in the 1990s. Other revenue (B) that includes fees, trading profits of fixed income securities, and foreign exchange operations, was about 3.5 trillion yen from 1995 until 1998. However, these figures exaggerate the underlying profitability of these activities because bond prices rose sharply under falling interest rates. I think that the underlying profitability of other revenue is probably about 2.5 trillion yen.

On the other hand, the operating cost has been declining over the past two years because of the cost-cutting measures by Japanese banks. Here again, I think that it is rather difficult to continue the recent pace of cost cutting. Certainly, Japanese banks may cut salaries and wages further by reducing employees and cutting average compensation. On the other hand, the computer system of Japanese banks is outdated. Banks could not invest in the system adequately because they have been preoccupied with bad-loan problems since the early 1990s. In the retail banking sector, banks cannot compete with national convenience store chains in payment services because banks cannot keep up with the sophisticated POS (point of sales) terminals of convenience shops.[5] Since banks have to invest

---

[5] In the *zengin* electronic fund transfer system, which is the main payment system among customers of banks, a user cannot send his name and messages in Chinese characters because the system cannot handle 2-byte codes. Because of the outdated bank-payment system, more and more cash payments are handled by convenience store chains rather than by banks.

TABLE 1

Profitability of Japanese Banking Sector, 1984–99
(Trillion yen)

Financial Year	1989	1990	1991	1992	1993	1994	1995	1996	1997	1998	1999	2000
Lending Margin (A)	7.5	7.1	8.9	9.8	9.2	9.7	10.8	10.7	10.0	9.6	9.7	9.4
Other Revenue (B)	2.5	2.6	2.2	2.5	2.8	2.1	3.3	3.7	3.6	3.1	2.5	3.0
Operating Costs (C)	6.6	7.1	7.5	7.7	7.7	7.8	7.8	8.0	8.0	7.5	7.3	7.1
Salaries and Wages	3.5	3.7	3.9	4.0	4.0	4.0	4.0	4.0	4.0	3.6	3.5	3.4
Gross Profit (D) = (A) + (B) − (C)	3.3	2.6	3.5	4.5	4.3	4.0	6.3	6.4	5.6	5.2	4.9	5.3
Loan Loss (E)	1.4	0.8	1.0	2.0	4.6	6.2	13.3	7.3	13.5	13.5	6.3	6.6
Net Operating Profit (F) = (D) − (E)	1.9	1.8	2.5	2.5	−0.4	−2.2	−7.0	−1.0	−7.9	−8.3	−1.4	−1.3
Realised Capital Gains (G)	2.8	2.0	0.7	0.0	2.0	3.2	4.4	1.2	3.6	1.4	3.8	1.4
Net Profit (F) + (G)	4.7	3.8	3.3	2.5	1.7	1.0	−2.6	0.2	−4.2	−6.9	2.3	0.1
Assets	943.6	927.6	914.4	859.5	849.8	845.0	848.2	856.0	848.0	759.7	737.2	804.3
Outstanding Loans (domestic banks)	424.3	445.8	460.3	472.3	477.8	482.7	482.3	477.9	472.6	463.4	456.9	

Notes:

Financial Statement of All Commercial Banks.

Other revenue (B) includes all other profit such as dealing profits and fees but excludes realised capital gains from stock and real estate holdings.

Realised capital gains includes gains from stock and real estate holdings.

Source: Japan Centre for Economic Research, *Monetary Policy Under Deflation* (March 2001, in Japanese).

heavily in information technology in the future, it will be difficult to cut total operating costs further.

Given these profit and cost figures, the gross profit before taking account of loan losses is about 5 trillion yen. On the other hand, the loan loss has exceeded the gross profit ever since FY 93. Since FY 94, the loan loss has been 6–14 trillion yen. Compared with the outstanding loan portfolio of about 500 trillion yen during this period, the loan loss rate has been 1.2–2.8 per cent. In other words, the Japanese banking sector has not been able to earn enough profit to cover loan losses. In cases when they reported the profit at the bottom line, this reflected realised capital gains on their stock and real estate holdings with low book values.

c. Weak Capital Position of the Japanese Banking Sector

Corresponding to these flow figures of profits, the capital position of Japanese banks has been deteriorating. Under the Japanese accounting rules on banks and the lenient application by the regulators, BIS capital ratios have been manipulated in many ways. Banks often used historical cost bookkeeping of equity portfolios, under-reserving against bad loans, and subordinated debts from friendly life-insurance companies so as to raise BIS ratios. As a result, most failed banks could maintain more than 8 per cent of BIS capital ratios until just before their bankruptcy.

I have tried to estimate simple leverage ratios of major banks and adjusted the simple core capital (tier 1 capital) by taking account of unrealised capital gains and losses. Table 2 shows the adjusted core capital/total asset ratios for major Japanese banks since 1998. In this estimation, I added unrealised capital gains and loan-loss reserves and subtracted the standardised estimated loan losses from the disclosed bad-loan figures. This particular estimate of capital is used because this variable worked well in predicting bank failures over a one-year time horizon with a regression model of various financial indicators.[6] According to this estimated distribution of core capital/asset ratio of banks, the leverage ratio fell to 0.93 per cent in March 1998. As many as eight banks had a negative equity position while only two banks were nationalised. The capital ratio recovered one year later by a 7.5 trillion yen capital injection by the Government. The capital ratio recovered further to 3.48 per cent by March 2000 as stock prices recovered. However, the ratio started to fall as banks continued to lose money due to bad loans and as stock prices started to fall again. By the end of February 2001, the capital ratio fell to 1.86 per cent.

As can be seen from Table 2, the capital position of banks is quite sensitive to stock prices. Although commercial banks show 36.7 trillion yen of capital on their balance sheet in the aggregate at the end of March 2001, this figure is inflated with 7.3 trillion yen of deferred tax assets (present value of future tax

---

[6] See Fukao and Japan Centre for Economic Research (2000a).

TABLE 2
Distribution of Adjusted Capital/Asset Ratio of Major Japanese Banks

		Number of Banks					Weighted Nikkei 225	
	Total	Less than −2%	−2% to 0%	0% to 2%	2% to 4%	4% to 6%	Average %	Index
March-98	19	2	6	8	3	0	0.93	16,527
March-99	17	0	2	10	5	0	2.07	15,837
March-00	17	0	0	4	9	4	3.48	20,337
September-00	15	0	0	5	10	0	2.36	15,747
March-01	15	1	0	8	6	0	1.83	12,883
September-01	15	1	3	11	0	0	0.86	9,774

Notes:
Adjusted Capital = Core Capital + Unrealised Capital Gains and Losses + Loan Loss Reserves − Estimated Loan Losses − Deferred Tax Asset.
Estimated Loan Losses = 100% of defaulted loans + 70% of risk loans + 20% of doubtful loans + 1% of normal loans.
Adjusted Capital/Asset Ratio = Adjusted Capital/Gross Asset.

Source: Japan Centre for Economic Research, *Monetary Policy Under Deflation* (March 2001, in Japanese).
The figures are updated by the author.

shelter) and 6.5 trillion yen of capital injection by the Government. Since banks pledge that they will repay the injected capital, the remaining net capital is only 22.9 trillion yen. This permanent capital is small compared with their stock portfolio of 44.5 trillion yen and their 68.2 trillion yen in problem loans.

Because the market value of stocks held by banks is about twice their net capital account, a 10 per cent fall in the stock-price index would wipe out 20 per cent of their net capital. In the late 1980s and early 1990s, the unrealised capital gain was very large, and they could withstand the fluctuations in stock prices. However, in the 1990s, banks gradually realised the gains so as to show paper profits to cover the huge loan losses. As a result, the unrealised capital gain was depleted when the Nikkei index of stock prices fell below 15,000 in late 2000.

d. Causes of the Unprofitable Banking Sector

The profit margin of Japanese banks is too small to cover the increased default risk since the collapse of *the bubble*. Many firms have not overcome their debt overhang and are surviving with the help of their banks. Banks have not succeeded in increasing their lending margin under strong competitive pressures from government-backed financial institutions. Moreover, under the terms and conditions of the Government capital injection in March 1999, banks are required to maintain and increase loans to small and medium sized firms. Because of this condition, banks often disregard the internal model-based required lending margin to make new loans to small companies. In the remainder of this section, I consider the effect of financial deregulation and the presence of Government-sponsored financial institutions on the profit margin of private banks.

(i) Effects of Deregulations

The average return on assets of Japanese banks was 1.84 per cent in FY 2000. On the other hand, the average funding cost was 0.28 per cent, and the average intermediation cost was 1.26 per cent. As a result, the lending spread was only 30 basis points. On the other hand, the annual loan-loss rate has been well over 1 per cent per year. Although a part of this negative profit margin is offset by other revenues such as trading profits and fees from customers, banks are making losses from their lending business (see Table 1).

One of the reasons for this low lending spread was the overhang of deposit-interest-rate controls until the early 1990s. When the Government controlled deposit-interest rates, banks could easily make money from deposit taking. On average, banks could get a 1.5 percentage point margin between the average funding rate and the short-term money market rate. The average lending rate was almost equal to short-term market rates. This fact probably indicates that banks passed a part of the regulatory rent of interest-rate control to borrowers. As the deposit-rate control was phased out in the late 1980s and early 1990s, banks tried to keep

FIGURE 1
Interest Rates and Inflation Rate, 1986–2000

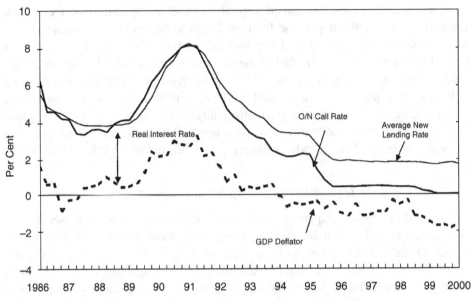

Note:
GDP deflator inflation rate is adjusted for changes in consumption tax rate in 1989 and 1997.

Source: Japan Centre for Economic Research, *Monetary Policy Under Deflation* (March 2001, in Japanese).

up their profit margin by increasing the lending rate relative to short-term market rates.

While banks have not raised their profit margins, borrowers are paying a higher interest rate in relation to the money market rate. Figure 1 shows the past movements of the average new lending rate, overnight call rate, and the GDP deflator-inflation rate. The gap between the interest rates and the inflation rate is the real interest rate. Reflecting loose monetary policy of the Bank of Japan, the real interest rate of the call rate has fallen from 1991 to 1998. On the other hand, the real interest rate and the new lending rate have not fallen much because of the increasing gap between the new lending rate and the call rate. While the opportunity cost of borrowing for large creditworthy companies is close to the call rate, the cost for small and medium sized companies is close to the new lending rate. Therefore, smaller companies experienced less of the expansionary effect of loose money policy than larger ones in the 1990s. This fact may have contributed to the relatively weak recovery of the small business sector in this decade.

(ii) Presence of government-sponsored financial institutions

In the Japanese financial markets, the presence of Government-sponsored financial institutions (GSFIs) is extremely large. Table 3 shows the market share

TABLE 3

Relative Size of Government-sponsored Financial Institutions, End of 2000

Loan	Asset Trillion Yen	Share Per Cent	GDP Ratio Per Cent
Government-sponsored agencies	163	26	32
Private banks	464	74	90
Total	627	100	122
Deposit			
Postal Saving System	255	34	50
Private banks	486	66	95
Total	741	100	144
Life Insurance (asset)			
Postal Life Insurance	119	40	23
Private life-insurance companies	180	60	35
Total	299	100	58

Source: Prepared by the author from data in the Bank of Japan, *Financial and Economic Statistics Monthly* (March 2001).

TABLE 4

Lending Rates of Government-sponsored Agencies, as of 9 February, 2001

Government Lending Agencies	Basic Loan Rate (Per Cent)	Average Terms (Years)
Japan Development Bank	2.05	16.7
People's Finance Corporation	2.05	7.3
Japan Finance Corporation for Small Business	2.05	8.9
Japan Finance Corporation for Municipal Enterprises	1.90	n.a.
Housing Loan Corporation	2.70	25.4

Note:
Loan rates are fixed.

Memorandum

Average Loan Rate of All Banks	2.12	Less than 1
Fixed Rate Housing Loan of Fuji Bank	4.65	20

Source: Japan Centre for Economic Research, *Monetary Policy Under Deflation* (March 2001, in Japanese).

of private banks and GSFIs at the end of year 2000. GSFIs have about one quarter of the loan market, one third of the deposit market, and 40 per cent of the life-insurance market.

In the loan market, GSFIs make very long-term loans at about a 2 per cent interest rate. They are especially dominant in the housing loan market, holding more than half of the outstanding housing loans. Table 4 shows the central lending rates of GSFIs on 9 February, 2001. While their new lending rates are similar to those of the short-term loans of private banks, the average term to maturity of GSFIs is much longer. Since Government agencies usually accept prepayments of their loans without penalties, their loans are more attractive to borrowers. While the market share of GSFIs in the loan market is smaller than in other markets, they have a 30–40 per cent share in rural prefectures. As a result, banks cannot set significantly higher lending rates over those of government agencies. Since Government agencies obtain subsidies of about 1 trillion yen per year as direct subsidy and indirect subsidy of zero-cost capital, they can cover the losses from credit and other risks in making loans. Compared with the outstanding domestic loans of GSFIs, this subsidy amounts to a 0.6 percentage point cost advantage relative to private financial institutions.[7]

In the deposit market, the Postal Saving System (PSS) is a dominant player. The deposits of the System are fully guaranteed by the Government. The deposit-interest rates are set competitively against those of private deposit-taking institutions. The PSS has more than 24,000 offices, and this branch network is by far the largest single financial institution in Japan. Even the largest private banking group, Mizuho, has only about 600 offices. Since the PSS does not charge an account-maintenance fee on customers, it is difficult for private banks to charge such a fee without alienating a large number of customers. Under the BOJ zero-interest rate policy, banks cannot get any profit margin between the zero-interest demand deposit and the market rate.

4. WEAK GOVERNANCE OF THE BANKING SECTOR

While I have investigated the reasons for the unprofitable banking sector, an important question still remains: Why don't banks stop unprofitable lending activities? In what follows, I suggest two hypotheses: absence of shareholder control; and the skewed incentive structure for bank management due to a negative equity position.

a. Absence of Control by Bank Shareholders

Although banks issued a large amount of preferred shares to the Government in March 1999, which diluted the ownership of existing shareholders, there was no public outcry of shareholders. In spite of the near collapse of major banks, all the shareholder meetings that approved the issuance of preferred shares to the Government were generally calm. No major shareholders objected to the deal. This is because the management of major banks is well protected by friendly

---

[7] See Higo (2001) on the role of GSFIs and their institutional details.

TABLE 5
Top Five Shareholders of Major Japanese Banks, End of September 2000

	1st	2nd	3rd	4th	5th
Mizuho Holdings	*Daiichi Life:* 4.1	*Nippon Life:* 2.7	Sumitomo Trust: 2.1	*Yasuda Life:* 2.0	*Asahi Life:* 1.9
Sakura Bank	*Mitsui Life:* 3.6	*Taiyo Life:* 3.6	*Nippon Life:* 3.6	State St.: 3.2	Chuo-Mitsui Trust: 3.0
Sumitomo Bank	*Sumitomo Life:* 4.5	*Nippon Life:* 4.0	Matsushita: 3.3	Sumitomo Trust: 2.4	Sanyo Electric: 2.0
Sumitomo Trust	*Sumitomo Life:* 2.5	State St.: 2.4	Sumitomo Bank: 2.2	Sumitomo Trust: 2.1	Mitsubishi Trust: 1.9
Bank of Tokyo Mitsubishi	*Meiji Life:* 5.0	*Nippon Life:* 3.6	Sumitomo Trust: 2.7	Tokyo Marine: 2.7	*Daiichi Life:* 2.5
Mitsubishi Trust	BOTM: 4.1	*Meiji Life:* 3.9	Mitsubishi Heavy: 2.7	Sumitomo Trust: 2.4	Asahi Glass: 2.2
Sanwa Bank	Toyo Trust: 4.1	*Nippon Life:* 4.0	Sumitomo Trust: 3.3	*Daido Life:* 3.0	*Meiji Life:* 2.7
Tokai Bank	Toyota: 5.0	*Chiyoda Life:* 3.7	*Nippon Life:* 3.0	Toyoshima: 2.4	*Daiichi Life:* 1.7
Asahi Bank	*Daiichi Life:* 4.1	*Chiyoda Life:* 3.2	*Yasuda Life:* 2.8	*Asahi Life:* 2.1	Sumitomo Trust: 2.0
Daiwa Bank	Nomura Sec: 3.2	*Tokyo Life:* 2.9	Fuji Fire Ins.: 2.6	Osaka Gas: 2.5	Nichido Fire Ins.: 1.8

Notes:
Italics are life-insurance companies. Bank of Tokyo Mitsubishi, BOTM. Chiyoda Life failed in October 2000 and Tokyo Life failed in March 2001.

Source: Nikkei Kaisha Joho (Spring 2001).

shareholders such as life-insurance companies and industrial companies. Table 5 shows the list of the top five shareholders of ten major Japanese banks. Out of 50 top shareholders in the list, 25 are life-insurance companies.

Since all major life-insurance companies are mutual companies, there is no formal cross-holding of shares. However, life-insurance companies often relied on banks to cultivate new corporate customers. Moreover, banks and life-insurance companies relied on each other to raise broadly defined capital. Banks provided subordinated credit and surplus notes to life-insurance companies amounting to 2.3 trillion yen at the end of March 2001.[8] On the other hand, life-insurance companies provided 5.1 trillion yen of subordinated credit to banks and own 5.4 trillion yen of bank stocks. Given this effective double gearing between the two, it is difficult to expect strong governance pressure on banks from life-insurance companies.

As mutual companies, the corporate governance structure of Japanese major life-insurance companies is also weak. In Japanese mutual life companies, a 'representative policyholders meeting' plays the role of a shareholders meeting in joint stock companies. Each representative policyholder has one equal vote. They are effectively chosen by the management themselves. Sometimes, they become policyholders after being asked to be representative policyholders by the management. In other cases, the managers of a company to which the insurance company has lent money are asked to become representative policyholders.

b. Skewed Incentive for Bank Management

Another possible reason for the lack of profits of Japanese banks is the skewed incentive structure for bank managers. In order to set the incentive structure right for corporate management and shareholders, it is necessary to maintain a significantly positive capital position. When there is no capital or a negative amount of capital, there is a skewed incentive for management to invest in excessively risky projects. Management would also try to conceal a negative equity position to keep control of the company and their jobs as long as possible.

As noted in Section 2, after the successive failure of some Japanese financial institutions, very large gaps between the before-failure and after-failure net asset values of banks were disclosed for the Hokkaido Takushoku Bank and Yamaichi Securities. Similarly, the Long-Term Credit Bank of Japan and Nippon Credit Bank were each found to have negative equity of more than 3 trillion yen after their failures.

In my judgment, the top management of most major banks knew that their banks were either insolvent or very marginally capitalised. Under such circumstances, the only safe exit from their positions was to keep their banks running

---

[8] Surplus notes of life-insurance companies are similar to non-voting redeemable preferred shares of ordinary companies.

without disclosing the reality; that is, postponing the recognition of bad loans. They had to comply with any irrational regulations by the FSA, including the requirement of making new loans to small and medium sized companies with very thin spread.

5. CONCLUSIONS

In this paper, I have tried to explain the cause of the lost decade of Japan as a difficulty of transition from the traditional Japanese governance system to a new one. This difficulty was compounded by a series of policy mistakes of creating a deflationary environment. The Japanese economy is stuck with a corporate sector without a traditional governance structure, coupled with a loss-making banking and insurance sector and rapidly increasing national debt. Moreover, a number of companies with negative equity are able to continue to operate because of extremely low interest rates, since the banks with little or no capital do not want to foreclose on these companies aggressively because it may trigger their own bankruptcy.

If the current pace of deflation and zero-interest rate policy are maintained, the Government is likely to have to subsidise the banking sector by 3–4 trillion yen a year indefinitely. In other words, the Government has to effectively national-ise most banks. Moreover, sooner or later, most life-insurance companies have to go to the bankruptcy court to obtain debt relief because they have promised a very high return on their long-term insurance policy without matching long-term high-yielding assets.

The Japanese economy now faces both micro- and macroeconomic problems. On the macro side, Japan is suffering from a gradually accelerating deflation and an unsustainable budget deficit. On the micro side, Japan has a loss-making banking sector with a long-lasting bad loan problem. Moreover, this micro-economic problem is exacerbated by the presence of large GSFIs with a strong political lobby.

In order to solve these complex simultaneous problems, both macro- and microeconomic policy tools need to be applied. Nominal interest rates should be raised by generating a mild inflation with a strong monetary expansion. In order to avoid rapid acceleration of the inflation rate, the BOJ should set an inflation target of about 0–3 per cent on the core consumer-price-index inflation rate. By stopping deflation, banks can raise nominal lending rates to obtain enough of a profit margin without raising real interest rates for customers. The Government has to abolish subsidies to GSFIs to allow private financial institutions to com-pete effectively. However, this policy package may have strong side effects. Resulting sharp declines in bond prices and higher nominal interest rates may wipe out many banks and insolvent companies. Banks had about 100 trillion yen of medium- and long-term bonds in early 2001. I estimate that the duration of yen-bond portfolios is about 2–4 years. If interest rates rise by 3 percentage points, the loss could be as high as 12 trillion yen. Thus, the only exit from this impasse is creative destruction with careful risk control.

REFERENCES

Bank for International Settlements (1993), *63rd Annual Report* (Basle).

Fukao, M. (2000), 'Recapitalizing Japan's Banks: The Functions and Problems of Financial Revitalization Act and Bank Recapitalization Act,' *Keio Business Review*, **38**, 1–16.

Fukao, M. and Japan Centre for Economic Research (eds.) (2000a), *Empirical Analysis of Financial Recession (Kinyu Fukyo no Jissho Bunseki)* (Nikkei Sinbun Sha: Tokyo, in Japanese).

Fukao, M. and Japan Centre for Economic Research (eds.) (2000b), *Examining Life Insurance Crisis (Kensho Seiho Kiki)* (Nikkei Sinbun Sha: Tokyo, in Japanese).

Higo, M. (2001), 'The Current State of FILP System: The Effects of 2001 Reform on the Functions of the FILP,' Bank of Japan Economic Research Department Working Paper 01-1 (March, in Japanese).

Horie, Y. (2001), *Economic Analysis of Lending Behavior* (Tokyo University Press, in Japanese).

Shigemi, Y. (1995), 'Asset Inflation in Selected Countries,' *Bank of Japan Monetary and Economic Studies*, **13**, 2, 89–130.

Index

accounting and auditing system   104–5
ageing population   70
Asahi Bank   115
Asian financial crisis   11, 20
asset prices   22–6
  bubble   100–1
  regulations, prudential   28–9
  taxation   30
  see also land prices; stock prices

bad loans   7, 20–1, 22, 32–3, 106–7
  financial system   100, 102–3, 104
  negative risk premium in interest rates   75,
    81, 88–92
  rational rigidity   36, 51, 57
Bank for International Settlements (BIS)   107,
  109
Banking Act (USA, 1933)   50
Banking Law   49
banking sector   99–100, 117–18
  balance sheets   8
  bubble, possibility of prevention   4
  community banking   7–8, 56–8:
    implications   42–50; paralysis of
    banks   50–6; theory   38–41
  convoy system of supervision   27
  credit ratings   103–4
  deregulation, corporate governance, and
    government-sponsored financial
    institutions   6–7
  financial crisis   102–6
  financial deregulations   6–7, 101–2,
    111–12
  governance, weak   114: absence of control
    by shareholders   114–16; skewed incentive
    for bank management   116–17
  international finance, domestic consequences
    of   5–6

Japan premium   104
negative risk premium in interest rates
  73–5, 94–5: low lending spreads and
  the share of bad loans in a portfolio
  88–92, 95–6; portfolio re-allocation in
  the liquidity trap   81–2; profitability
  of new bank lending   82–8; public
  financial intermediation   92–4;
  theory   75–81
problems   18, 22
profits *see* profits, banks
rational rigidity   35–8, 56–8: implications
  42–50; paralysis of banks   50–6;
  theory   38–41
reform   13
regulations   27–9
USA   11
weakness   206: bad-loan situation   106–7;
  capital position   109–11; causes of
  unprofitability   111–14;
  profitability   107–9
Bank of Japan (BOJ)   14
  bad loans   103
  banking crisis   35
  bubble   26–7: asset prices and monetary
    policy   22, 25; prevention, possibility
    of   2–3, 4, 14
  exchange rate stability   9
  inflation target   117
  international finance, domestic
    consequences of   5
  liquidity trap   74
  monetary policy   22, 25, 101, 112
  negative risk premium in interest rates   81
  price expectations, changing   9–10, 11
  zero-interest policy   100, 114
Bank of Tokyo Mitsubishi   115
Bank Recapitalisation Act   105–6

bankruptcy
    community banking   42, 44–8, 57
    fiscal reconstruction movements   69
Basle II   28
Basle Committee on Banking Supervision   28
Basle rule   28
bequest tax   30–1
Bergsten, C. Fred   3
bond-dependency rate   59–60
bonds, government
    fiscal policy   59–60: sustainability   64–5
    international finance, domestic
        consequences of   6
    negative risk premium in interest rates:
        profitability of new bank lending   88;
        theory   75
    price expectations, changing   10–11
bubble period   1–2, 14, 17–22, 33
    asset prices and monetary policy   22–6
    as cause of lost decade   32–3
    macroeconomic aspects   22–7
    prevention, possibility of   2–4, 14
    problems in the 1990s   4: community
        banking and structural change   7–8;
        deregulation, corporate governance,
        and government-sponsored financial
        institutions   6–7; fiscal policy,
        ineffective   4–5; international finance,
        domestic consequences   5–6
    regulations, prudential   27–9
    securities   32
    tax issues   29–31
budget deficits, optimal   66–8
Bundesbank   2, 26, 27, 33

call market   105
capital gains tax   30, 32, 101
capitalisation
    international finance, domestic
        consequences of   5–6
    weak position of banking sector   109–11
commercial paper   87

community banking   7–8, 56–8
    implications   42–50
    paralysis of banks   50–6
    theory   38–41
consumption tax   11–12, 69
corporate governance   6–7, 116
currency taxation   12
current account   78, 79

Daiwa Bank   115
deflation   18, 21
demographic factors   70
Deposit Insurance Corporation   35, 105
Deposit Insurance Law   106
deregulation of financial sector   7, 101–2,
        111–12
discount rate   2–3, 27, 33
dividends, taxation   30

equity prices *see* stock prices
exchange rates   9
exports   69

Federal Reserve
    inflation   22
    interest rates   2, 26, 27, 33
    post-World War II situation   11
Financial Revitalisation Act   105, 106
Financial Services Agency (FSA)   107, 117
financial system   99–100, 117–18
    asset prices and monetary policy   24–5
    deregulations   7, 101–2, 111–12
    government-sponsored institutions   7–8,
        99–100, 112–14: market share   112–13;
        negative risk premium in interest
        rates   92–4; subsidies   13, 117
    real estate bubble and financial crisis   100–6
    reform   13
    regulations   27–9, 33
    see also bad loans; banking sector
Fiscal Investment and Loan Programme
        (FILP)   99

fiscal policy 59–60, 70–2
  bubble as cause of lost decade 33
  budget deficits, optimal 66–8
  Hashimoto Administration, reconstruction
    movements 68–70
  ineffective 4–5
  Keynesian effect, evaluation 60–4
  price expectations, changing 10
  resolving Japan's problems 8
  sustainability, fiscal 64–6, 71–2
  see also tax
Fiscal Structural Reform Act (1997) 60, 68,
  70
foreign assets 78–81
foreign direct investment (FDI) 80–1
France 50

Germany
  banking sector 50
  Bundesbank 2, 26, 27, 33
  stock prices 27
government debt *see* public debt
government solvency 64–6
government-sponsored institutions 7–8,
  99–100, 112–14
  market share 112–13
  negative risk premium in interest rates
    92–4
  subsidies 13, 117
Greenspan, Alan 25
gross domestic product (GDP) 1, 18, 20

Hale, David 3–4
Hashimoto Administration 68–70
Hokkaido Takushoku Bank 35, 104, 116
Hong Kong 29
housing loan companies (*jusen*) 21, 33, 99,
  102, 103–4
Housing Loan Corporation 92–3, 103

Industrial Bank of Japan (IBJ) 37, 49
industrial dynamics 52–3

inflation 21–2, 22
  bubble 19, 22, 26: asset prices and monetary
    policy 22, 24, 25–6; possibility of
    prevention 3
  deflation 18, 21
  financial system 100, 117:
    deregulations 112
  price expectations, changing 9, 11, 12
information technology (IT)
  banks 107–9
  stocks 21, 25
inheritance tax 30–1, 101
interest rates 22, 33
  bubble 26–7: asset prices and monetary
    policy 23; possibility of prevention 2, 3
  financial system 100, 117: deregulations
    111–12
  international finance, domestic
    consequences of 5–6
  negative risk premium 73–5, 94–5: low
    lending spreads and share of bad loans in a
    bank's portfolio 88–92, 95–6; portfolio
    re-allocation in the liquidity trap 81–2;
    profitability of new bank lending 82–8;
    public financial intermediation 92–4;
    theory 75–81
  price expectations, changing 9, 12
international finance, domestic consequences
  of 5–6

Japan premium 104, 105, 106
jusen (housing loan companies) 21, 33, 99,
  102, 103–4

keiretsu firms 37
Keynesian effect, fiscal policy 60–4
Koizumi Administration 13, 70
Komeitō 12
Kurosawa, Hiroshi 49

land prices
  bubble 27, 100–1, 102: possibility of

prevention   4
community banking   50–1
fluctuations   1, 2, 17–20, 32–3, 102–3
regulations, prudential   29
taxes   31
see also real estate sector
land tax   31
learning-by-doing, and rational rigidity
   39–40
Liberal Democratic Party (LDP)
   Bank of Japan's purchase of government
      bonds   10
   Emergency Economic Package   105
   fiscal policy   60
life-insurance companies   7, 116
liquidity trap   73–4, 81, 95
   portfolio re-allocation   81–2, 83
loan dependency ratio   91
local allocation tax system   70
Long-Term Credit Bank   104, 105, 116
   nationalisation   35, 105
Louvre Accord   2, 26

Ministry of Finance (MOF)   14
   bad loans   103
   bubble: possibility of prevention   3, 4, 14;
      regulations, prudential   29
   deregulated banking sector   7
   Emergency Economic Package   105
   financial system   99
   fiscal policy   59–60: ineffective   4
   international finance, domestic
      consequences of   5
   jusen crisis   103–4
Mitsubishi Trust   115
Miyazawa-Baker announcement   26
Mizuho Holdings   114, 115
monetary policy
   bubble   18, 22–6, 101: as cause of lost
      decade   33
   exchange rate stability   9
   international finance, domestic

consequences of   5
price expectations, changing   9, 12:
   printing money   10–11
   resolving Japan's problems   8, 9
mortgage interest payment deductibility   29
mutual-life-insurance companies   7, 116

negative risk premium   73–5, 94–5
   low lending spreads and share of bad loans
      in a bank's portfolio   88–92, 95–6
   portfolio re-allocation in the liquidity
      trap   81–2
   profitability of new bank lending   82–8
   public financial intermediation   92–4
   theory   75–81
Nippon Credit Bank   104, 116
   nationalisation   35, 105
Nishikawa, President of Sumitomo Mitsui
   Bank   37
Nishimura, Masao   37
non-performing loans *see* bad loans

Obuchi, Prime Minister   60

Postal Saving System (PSS)   94, 114
price-dividend ratio   23
price expectations, changing   9–10
private consumption
   fiscal reconstruction movements   68–9
   Keynesian effect   61–2, 63, 64
private investment
   Keynesian effect   62, 63, 64
   negative risk premium in interest rates   94
profits, banks   100, 107–9
   causes of unprofitability   111: deregulations
      111–12; government-sponsored
      financial institutions   112–14
   community banking   43–4, 49–50, 51, 57
   low lending spreads and bad loans   89
   new loans   82–8
   public financial intermediation   92
public debt   8

fiscal policy 60: fiscal reconstruction movements 69; ineffective 5; optimal budget deficits 66–8
  price expectations, changing 10, 11
  sustainability 22, 64–6
public financial intermediation 92–4
public investment 61–3
public opinion
  on financial crisis 103
  on role of government 70

rational rigidity 35–8, 56–8
  implications 42–50
  institutionalisation 42, 48–50
  paralysis of banks 50–6
  theory 38–41
real estate sector
  bubble: origin 100–2; possibility of prevention 3–4
  community banking 50, 56
  inheritance tax 30–1
  international finance, domestic consequences of 5
  regulations 28, 29
  taxes 30–1
  see also land prices
rents, taxation 30
representation policy holders meetings 116
Resolution Trust Corporation 94–5
risk premium, negative 73–5, 94–5
  low lending spreads and share of bad loans in a bank's portfolio 88–92, 95–6
  portfolio re-allocation in the liquidity trap 81–2
  profitability of new bank lending 82–8
  public financial intermediation 92–4
  theory 75–81

Sakura Bank 115
Sanwa Bank 115
Sanyo Securities 35, 104
scrip, government-issued 12

shareholders, absence of control by 114–16
Sony 37
stock prices
  of banks 105
  Basle rule 28
  Black Monday (USA) 26
  bubble 23, 100–1
  and capital position of banks 109–11
  community banking 50
  fluctuations 1, 17, 19–20, 32, 102
  information technology 21, 25
  taxes 32
Sumitomo Bank 115
Sumitomo Mitsui Bank 37
Sumitomo Trust 115
Sumitomo Trust and Banking 105

tax 31
  bequest 30–1
  capital gains 30, 32, 101
  consumption 11–12, 69
  currency 12
  distortions 101
  dividend 30
  fiscal reconstruction movements 68, 69, 70
  inheritance 30–1, 101
  Keynesian effect 63–4
  land 31
  mortgage interest payment deductibility 29
  rents 30
  securities 32
  smoothing 66
Tokai Bank 115
Toyota 37

unemployment 21
United States of America
  1990s 2, 14
  Banking Act (1933) 50
  bankruptcy 44–5

Black Monday   26, 101
Federal Reserve: inflation   22; interest
    rates   2, 26, 27, 33; post-World War II
    situation   11
information technology bubble   25
interest rates   6, 73–4, 75–7, 81
international finance, domestic
    consequences of   6
Japanese *bubble*, possibility of
    prevention   3
lending spreads   91
post-World War II situation   11
profitability of new bank lending   85–7

Resolution Trust Corporation   94–5
stock prices   27
see also yen/dollar exchange rate

Yamaichi Securities   35, 104, 116
yen/dollar exchange rate
    bubble   26
    domestic consequences of international
        finance   6
    negative risk premium in interest rates
        76–7, 95
    stabilisation   9, 95